Say what you mean, mean what you say

Coming to grips with children's inappropriate behaviour

Colophon

Say What You Mean, Mean What You Say is available via Lightning Source.
The reader can find answers to questions about the book, or aspects of inappropriate behaviour in children or adolescents at the website www.saywhatyoumean.nl. Questions are usually addressed in short films in the Q & A section. The classification of the films follows the structure of the manual.

Publisher: Uitgeverij De Merel, The Netherlands
Author: Michiel Noordzij
Translation: Kristine Kohlstrand
Layout: Leiden in vorm! Gerard Gerritsma
Photography: Marc de Haan
Production: Lightning Source -POD
With thanks to: Evi, Nick, Sa Xi, Tobias

ISBN/EAN 978-90-820091-0-1

Copyright © 2012, Uitgeverij De Merel
All rights reserved. No part of this publication may be reproduced, stored in a retrieval system or transmitted in any form or by any means, electronic, photocopying or otherwise, without the permission of the publisher.

This book has been compiled with the greatest possible care. Neither the editor nor the publisher accept any liability for any inaccuracies and/or errors it may contain.

Is this the book for you?

This is a book about dealing with children's behavioural problems, written with parents, teachers and childcare workers in mind. Is this the book for you? Even if you are not a parent, a teacher or a childcare worker, but a grandmother, aunt, sports trainer or youth leader? Is this a book for the child who does not have serious behavioural problems? There is a good chance that it is, because **Say what you mean, mean what you say** was written for anyone who has anything to do with children. For anyone who cares about children, and wants to understand and help them, regardless of how difficult and challenging their behaviour may be at times.

Say what you mean, mean what you say was written by a child psychiatrist who trains adults to work with children and adolescents with behavioural problems. What is the best way of dealing with seriously inappropriate behaviour? This book provides valuable help and support for those who are involved with these young people at any level. This programme will help them to find appropriate solutions for dealing with problem situations and avoiding escalations.

The programme is also suitable for less serious behavioural problems. Parents who are dealing with a healthy but temperamental toddler or an ordinary but obstinate teenager will find this book just as helpful. It will help you to come to grips with the educational situation even when doors are being slammed and voices raised in anger. It provides practical advice for every family or classroom.

So, in answer to your question: yes, this is definitely the book for you.

Foreword

Defiant behavior by children toward their parents is probably the most common management problem of child-rearing faced by modern parents and is certainly among the most common referral complaints of parents whose children are seen at child psychiatric and psychology clinics. Clear, brief, science-based recommendations for parents are essential for parents seeking treatment for their children because time is of the essence. Defiant child behavior can become ingrained and later extrapolated to impaired social interactions with peers, teachers, and other adults in community settings and very difficult to ameliorate after 12 years of age. I am very pleased to see that such is the content of this fine book on child behavior management of difficult children by Dr. Noordzij. Many trade books exist to give parents advice on raising their children but most are based on the mere opinion of the author and whatever clinical wisdom they may have gained from their experience, if any. But clinical wisdom alone is not always scientifically accurate and can often be misleading when dealing with specific age groups, special populations or ethnic groups outside of the experiences of that clinician-author. That is why such books as this one are so important. They contain far more empirically-tested recommendations for parents applicable across a wider age range and the general population thus having a far greater likelihood of actually addressing the problems parents are encountering with their children. Just as positive is the approach of Dr. Noordzij to skip the use of professional jargon and clinical diagnoses unnecessary to advise parents on the most effective management methods to employ with their children. This frees this book of the stilted and pedantic language not to mention the arrogance that can be found in other trade books on this topic.

The focus on teaching parents about proactive, reactive, and post-active components of sound child behavior management is especially refreshing and likely to maximize the effectiveness of training. It does so by showing parents that there are effective ways to *preclude* the occurrence of defiant behavior rather than the more commonly known reactive methods for what to do when such behavior does occur. And the special focus on post-active components is, to my knowledge, unique to this program giving both parent and child a clear understanding of the time course of the consequences being invoked and adjusted to the developmental level of the child. My compliments to Dr. Noordzij for writing this smart, sensible, scientifically-grounded, and effective program for helping parents to manage their defiant child.

Russell A. Barkley, Ph.D.
Clinical Professor of Psychiatry and Pediatrics
Medical University of South Carolina
Charleston, SC, USA

Author of: *Your Defiant Child, Your Defiant Teen, Defiant Children: A Clinician's Manual for Assessment and Parent Training,* and *Defiant Teens: A Clinician's Manual for Assessment and Family Training*

Instructions for use

In this book, a behavioural problem is said to exist if a child frequently acts in a way that he should not or frequently fails to behave how he should.

This manual describes a method that adults can use to come to grips with some serious behavioural problems found in young children and adolescents. It sets out a systematic approach to dealing with inappropriate behaviour. It trains you, the reader, and in that respect its focus is on training the trainers.

These trainers, or future trainers, are all adults dealing with the behavioural problems of children on the "shop floor", such as parents, teachers and childcare workers. Perhaps you have become a trainer against your will. You have tried everything else and reached the limits of your ability to deal with the child. Nothing you have learned ever seems to work. You often find yourself in a position where you feel angry, powerless, and disappointed with the child. The child and his or her behavioural problem have taken over the educational situation.

This is a six-step programme. The structure of the programme takes into account the difficult position in which the adult and the child find themselves. The first step involves mapping out this unpleasant situation. The second step describes how you, the adult, can take back control. The third step of the programme focuses on developing an action plan (which we refer to as the *intervention*). The next three steps describe in practical terms how the intervention is carried out. The intervention is spread out over three moments in time: before, during and after an incident.

The programme's six steps are described in six chapters. The chapters have the same structure. Each one begins with a brief introduction to the step covered by the chapter. This is followed by sections containing *instructions* and *explanations*. The instructions are listed under "Do the following", while explanations are headed "Consider the following". The sections can be read separately or as a whole. Each section is preceded by two *portraits*, one of a younger child and one of an older child. The portraits make it easier to visualize the instructions that follow.

The appendix at the back of the book defines terms such as *intervention, sanction, functioning level* and *growth-promoting language*. It also includes metaphors discussed in the main text. In addition, the appendix contains ten portraits of younger and older children. They are designed to help you gain an understanding of the complex situations that can arise on the shop floor as well as suggestions for dealing with the behavioural problem. The table of contents provides a summary of the training instruction. The Quick Reference Section at the end of the book offers a brief overview and a mind map of the entire programme.

The writing style is affirmative, and the reader is addressed as "you". We refer to the child as "he" (which is understood to include "she") and not as "it". The book is designed to be used in real-life situations.
In time you will be able to use this manual as a practical reference work. The book is also highly suitable for use in professional educational settings.

Table of contents

1. Map out the situation — 9
- 1.1. Give a general description of the inappropriate behaviour — 12
  - a. Identifying the source of frustration — 13
  - b. Describing the course of behaviour over time — 13
- 1.2. Describe your current response and emotions — 14
  - a. Reviewing the role of the child in the problem — 15
  - b. Reviewing the role of the adults in the problem — 16
  - c. Reviewing the role of the environment in the problem — 17
- 1.3. Ask yourself who is in charge — 19
  - a. Reviewing the role of the child — 19
  - b. Reviewing the role of the adult — 20
- 1.4. Describe your concerns and hopes — 21
  - a. Checking short-term consequences — 21
  - b. Checking long-term consequences — 22
- 1.5. Determine whether the current situation can be allowed to continue — 23
  - a. Drawing conclusions — 24
  - b. Setting a time limit — 24
  - c. Setting a limit with regard to an acceptable level of functioning — 24

2. Fix your own attitude first — 27
- 2.1. Identify your attitude — 30
  - a. Drawing a distinction between your attitude and the work floor — 32
  - b. Identifying the vicious circle — 32
- 2.2. Go from passive to active — 34
  - a. Accepting the chronic nature of the problems — 36
  - b. Redefining unwillingness as inability — 37
  - c. Going from waiting to starting a project — 38

3. Prepare the intervention — 41
- 3.1. Choose the behaviour that needs to change — 44
  - a. Making a list — 45
  - b. Choosing a category and subcategory — 46
  - c. Determining the level of functioning — 46
- 3.2. Design the intervention — 49
  - a. Basing the intervention on the level of functioning — 51
  - b. Timing the intervention — 51
  - c. Shaping the intervention — 52

4.	**Hold a work session using growth-promoting language**	**57**
	4.1. Announce the work session	60
	a. Inviting the child	61
	b. Determining the conditions	61
	4.2. Hold the work session	63
	a. Using growth-promoting language	64
	b. Giving a brief explanation of your reasons	64
	c. Announcing the sanction	65
	4.3. Conclude the work session	67
	a. Being prepared for resistance	67
	b. Staying in control	68
5.	**Apply the sanction**	**71**
	5.1. Give the announced sign	74
	a. Avoiding delay	74
	b. Avoiding further discussion	74
	5.2. Apply the sanction calmly and professionally	75
	a. Meaning what you say	76
	b. Avoiding an angry response	76
	c. Sticking to the time schedule	77
	5.3. Deal with new inappropriate behaviour	78
	a. Dealing with the child's contribution to the problem	79
	b. Dealing with the adult's contribution to the problem	80
6.	**Use growth-promoting language to evaluate the intervention**	**83**
	6.1. Be aware of the need to hold an appraisal	86
	a. Recognising the appraisal as part of the programme	87
	b. Understanding the advantages of the appraisal	87
	6.2. Maintain an active work attitude	88
	a. Staying alert	89
	b. Using the coaching model	89
	c. Understanding the power of repetition	90
	6.3. Discuss the child's reaction to the sanction in growth-promoting language	91
	a. Avoiding the you-bin	91
	b. Using positive wording	92
	6.4. Link one practice situation to the next	93
	a. Making the post-active appraisal pro-active	94
	b. Maintaining focus	94

Appendices   97

A. The Intervention   99
B. The Sanction   105
C. The Metaphors   111
D. The portraits   117
E. Quick Reference Section   131

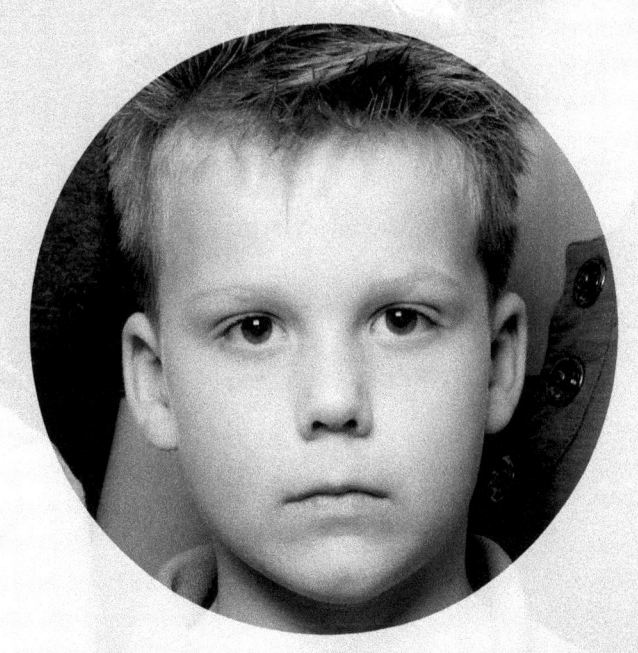

1. Map out the situation

1. MAP OUT THE SITUATION

1. Map out the situation

- **1.1.** Give a general description of the inappropriate behaviour
  - **1.1.a.** Identifying the source of frustration
  - **1.1.b.** Describing the course of behaviour over time
- **1.2.** Describe your current response and emotions
  - **1.2.a.** Reviewing the role of the child in the problem
  - **1.2.b.** Reviewing the role of the adults in the problem
  - **1.2.c.** Reviewing the role of the environment in the problem
- **1.3.** Ask yourself who is in charge
  - **1.3.a.** Reviewing the role of the child
  - **1.3.b.** Reviewing the role of the adult
- **1.4.** Describe your concerns and your hopes
  - **1.4.a.** Checking short-term consequences
  - **1.4.b.** Checking long-term consequences
- **1.5.** Determine whether the current situation can be allowed to continue
  - **1.5.a.** Drawing conclusions
  - **1.5.b.** Setting a time limit
  - **1.5.c.** Setting a limit with regard to an acceptable level of functioning

What is this chapter about?

If a child has serious behavioural problems you have probably searched everywhere for a solution. You probably feel you are caught in a circle of disappointment, anger and powerlessness. An unfamiliar, difficult situation has arisen which can no longer be dealt with by a few simple tips. This chapter helps you to map out this situation.

1. Map out the situation

Portrait of a younger child
"You're in my space!"

It drives Jill crazy. Sometimes she longs to send her three children to their rooms and lock the doors. She hates feeling like this. Parents are supposed to love their children and be patient, but that is very difficult when you have to be on your guard at all times. The children are constantly at each other's throats. Especially Josh, who is six, and Amy, who is five. They are always far too rough with two-year old Paul or making him cry.

Do other people have these problems? Jill feels she might be the only mother who cannot control her children. She has tried everything. This time she tries reasoning with them. When she asks her children, "When Daddy comes home tonight, wouldn't it be nice if we could all sit down together at the table without fighting?", Josh and his sister agree that it would. Little Paul does not participate in this conversation. But when the shouting starts, he shouts too.

Jill has barely finished speaking when Amy shouts at Josh, who is sitting next to her at the table. "You're in my space!" Amy cries. Her hand traces a vertical dividing line in the air, and Josh is forbidden to cross it. Jill tries again: "What did I just say? You promised to be good but less than a minute later you are already fighting again!" Amy angrily plants her elbows on the table and declares, "Josh is stupid! He's the stupidest brother ever!" Before Jill can respond, Josh jabs his little sister with his elbow. Jill loses her patience and drags Josh away from the table. She pulls open the door, causing the glass panes to shake, and pushes Josh into the hall, shouting, "Get out of my sight!" Josh is frightened, but he quickly recovers from the shock. "She started it!" he retorts. As Jill closes the door, Josh hears his sister chant, "Nah nah na-nah nah!"

Jill makes various threats, including telling Santa. When her husband gets home he is tired. Jill thinks he is too strict with the children. He thinks Jill should just be more consistent with them, and that no should mean no. "That's easy for you to say, you're not around them all day!" she retorts. "I know," he answers, "but somebody has to go out and earn a living."

Portrait of an older child
"The repeat offender"

Nathan's parents are at the end of their tether. Nathan is going to spend his holiday at a friend's house and will not be allowed to stay at home. His parents decided this after the last time they went on holiday. Nathan had been allowed to stay home alone for a fortnight. He left a huge mess behind in the kitchen, cigarettes had been stubbed out on the living room floor, and the drinks cabinet had been raided.

His parents have now decided that although Nathan does not have to come to France with them, he cannot stay home alone. Nathan thinks this is ridiculous and childish. His father wants to arrange for him to go to a camp, but Nathan refuses. He thinks camp is totally lame. He would, however, like to have the money his father was prepared to spend on sending him to camp. As the holidays approach, his parents see that Nathan is not making any attempt to find a place to stay. He is letting matters take their course. At the last minute, when he finally realises that his parents really are going to lock him out of the house when they leave, he arranges to stay with friends of the family.

After their holiday Nathan's parents notice a broken window in the cellar. It is clear that Nathan has been in the house. There are remnants of sandwiches, an open jar of peanut butter and a melted packet of butter. Someone has been through the house, apparently looking for money. When he is confronted, Nathan adamantly denies this. Later he says that William's internet connection was down and he needed to check his e-mails. He takes no responsibility for his actions. "It was your decision that I couldn't stay, not mine!" he retorts. He is not bothered about the broken window and the fact that the house had not been secure for days. His parents feel their hearts sink.

Introduction

The first chapter helps you to take stock of the situation regarding the child's behaviour. Use checklist points 1.1 to 1.5 (see below) to do this. Taking stock of the situation helps you become more aware of what happens between you and the child. Creating a little distance can help. The second aim of this chapter is to convince you that it is necessary to intervene.

A child's behaviour can relapse, and as the adult in the situation, you may also have doubts about the effectiveness of your intervention. In either case, you should go through the checklist again. If you have already followed all six steps of the programme, the objective of going through the checklist again is to chart your progress. If you have already followed all of the steps in the programme several times and your chosen strategy does not seem to work, you should re-evaluate the child's level of functioning (see 3.1.c).

Bear in mind that this programme teaches you a systematic approach to dealing with inappropriate behaviour. Discussing matters with the child is no longer an option, nor is using rewards as incentives for good behaviour. Those strategies work for minor behavioural problems. The problems you now face are more serious, and the sense of impotence and frustration is much greater.

1.1. Give a general description of the inappropriate behaviour

Portrait of a younger child

The first step is to describe the frustration the adult feels. Josh, Amy and Paul's mother doesn't know where to start. The portrait shows that there are many behavioural problems that frustrate her; the list is long. She cannot tackle all of them at once, but she can describe what annoys her. The descriptions can take the form of separate phrases listed in no particular order. You can compare this to a brainstorming session. From your list of individual phrases you can pick specific behaviours to focus on.

Portrait of an older child

If someone asked you to give a general description of Nathan's behaviour you could simply say that things have been going wrong for a long time. It seems impossible to hold him to his word. He makes promises, but never keeps them.

Why would you want to describe this in detail? The answer to that question is the starting point of this book. Once you, as parents, start to describe the pattern of Nathan's inappropriate behaviour over time, you will realise that you have been muddling along for years. You can see how difficult it is to hold Nathan to his word, and are aware of the extent of your efforts to build yours confidence in him. You can feel the fatigue of all the disappointment, and the anger this causes. You notice just how powerless you have become in dealing with Nathan's behavioural problems. But you may also become aware of the method you have tended to use. A method of approaching the problem which you are now forced to conclude was ineffective, or worked only briefly.

Start by formulating what it is about the child's behaviour that frustrates you. Then try to describe the course of that behaviour over time.

1.1.a. Identifying the source of frustration

Do the following:
- Try to identify the inappropriate behaviour. Describe exactly what it is that bothers you. You can express your own frustration and disappointment. You can also write something about the behaviour you would have liked to have seen.
- Describe the frustration you feel towards the child's behaviour but also say something about yourself and the way other adults approach the problem.
- When you repeat the steps in the programme, describe which aspects of behaviour have improved and which are still a source of frustration.

1.1.b. Describing the course of behaviour over time

Do the following:
- Describe how the child's inappropriate behaviour has developed over time. Use the following checklist:
  - When did it begin?
  - When did it become noticeable, frustrating, insufferable or unacceptable?
  - Is the behaviour always present, or does it crop up periodically or at specific times?
  - In which situations is it most prevalent?
  - When is the behaviour absent?

Consider the following:
The purpose of this description is to raise awareness. You will become aware of the need to deal with the child's inappropriate behaviour. You can describe the behaviour in general terms. The description will become more detailed as the programme develops. You may find that it is not always easy to pinpoint exactly what it is that frustrates you, but you can add to the description later on.

Frustration can arise in various ways. It may be that you have tried several tactics, but none of them seems to work well enough. It may also be the case that while you have so far done little about the child's behaviour, others – neighbours, school, a sports club – have now forced you to face up to it. You may notice that you are walking on eggshells to keep the situation from escalating. It is possible that you may have noticed the behavioural problem in the past, but are only now realising that half-measures no longer work. It is not uncommon to see adults divided in their response to the behavioural problem. One of them may be dismayed by the lack of support or action on the part of another, who in turn may be annoyed by the other's exaggerated concern.

A child's behaviour usually develops into inappropriate behaviour gradually. Sometimes the process goes almost unnoticed. Along the way you may have become stricter than you want to be, or more tolerant than you would like. There comes a time when you realise that the behavioural problem has been around for a while. Having to identify precisely how long can provide valuable insight. The realisation that the inappropriate behaviour has existed for a long time can prompt you to change the way you deal with it. Evidently, the inappropriate behaviour is not going to go away on its own.

- Mapping out the course of a behavioural problem is a useful exercise. Later on it can help you to deal with the problem in a more targeted and effective manner. For example, it may be that:
  - the inappropriate behaviour happens in a group, but not in one-on-one situations;
  - it happens only at school, but not at home;
  - it is worse in the morning than it is in the evening;
  - it occurs mostly when the father is not at home;
  - it is mostly directed at a particular child;
  - it happens only in unstructured situations;
  - it did not start until puberty

Keep in mind that you can follow the steps in the cycle described in this programme several times. Each time a session will follow during which you can evaluate whether or not you are on the right track. If the behaviour you decided to tackle has improved, you can choose something else to work on. But you may also find that the approach you have chosen has not led to an improvement. You then have to describe the new situation.

1.2. Describe your current response and emotions

Portrait of a younger child

Jill starts with Josh's behaviour. It turns out that she has written much more about him than about Amy. Outside of the family, Amy functions perfectly normally. Jill writes down Josh's role in all of the emotions surrounding his behaviour.

Josh is quick to pick fights with the other members of his new football team. He already thinks the trainer is stupid. Jill notes that is impossible to talk to him about his behaviour. She observes carefully and notes that Amy and Paul usually play quietly together. But once Josh comes home, someone starts crying within five minutes. Jill walks on eggshells when her husband is at home. He is much more direct and strict with Josh. He frequently sends him away from the table. Josh's response is, "I don't care anyway." That makes her husband even angrier. He scolds him for talking back and sometimes even spanks him. Poor Josh! If Jill objects to this, she and her husband start to quarrel and blame one another. That is why Jill has started letting Josh eat before the others. At least then she can avoid weekday confrontations between Josh and her husband. She'll take care of it herself.

In the supermarket, Josh tosses a big bag of sweets into the trolley even though Jill has forbidden it. She tries to be firm, but Josh throws a huge tantrum. A woman she barely knows sees what's happening and smirks, "Just let him spend a week with me!" Jill also remembers that her mother recently said that the children were too wild for her to babysit.

Portrait of an older child

When Nathan's parents are asked to describe their current emotions, there is almost no stopping them. During the process of writing them down they realise that Nathan's behaviour has dominated the family for quite a few years. Since puberty, he has become more and more unapproachable. He lies when it serves his purposes, but he can also be very sweet when he needs something. He is often very rude to his mother. If they ask him for help, he suddenly has homework. But when they ask him if he has homework to do, he always says he has done it. His bleary eyes tell his parents he is smoking cannabis. His parents find little plastic bags in his room. At first he says he was keeping the pot for a friend, but soon he cannot even be bothered to lie. Of course his father was so boring when he was young he would never have dared do anything bad, but Nathan is no nerd. The parents have each developed their own responses. They are no match for Nathan's verbal abuse. They realise that they give in just to keep him from badgering them. Nathan's mother accuses his father of failing to intervene when Nathan is shouting at her. And now, since they are on the subject, Nathan's father accuses his wife of coming between him and his son precisely when he had decided to intervene.

Others have also reacted to Nathan's behaviour since he was involved in an incident where the windows of a bus shelter were smashed. To his great dismay, he was forced to do twenty hours of supervised community service picking up litter and rubbish at the railway station. And his behaviour was the reason why he was held back at school last year.

Inappropriate behaviour often involves an intense interaction between the child and adults. Each party is dissatisfied with the behaviour and attitude of the other. Others besides the child and parents may express their unhappiness.

Use the three checklists below to help you formulate experiences and interactions.

1.2.a. Reviewing the role of the child in the problem

Do the following:
- Realise that in the case of seriously inappropriate behaviour, the child can behave like an 'unreasonable tyrant'.
- Check whether the child shows any of the following behaviours. Add to the list if necessary.
  - Pesters and nags to get his own way.
  - Seems to be insatiable.
  - Is unfazed by all criticism.
  - Seems untouched by punishment. Nothing bothers him (*"Whatever..."*).
  - Does not seem to learn anything from more severe forms of punishment.
  - Responds to punishment or a sanction with, "I don't care."
  - Goes his own way, paying little or no attention to you.
  - Lies outright.
  - Does exactly what he wants to do.
  - Gives you the feeling that your house is nothing but a hotel.
  - Gets angry almost immediately when spoken to.
  - Plays parents and other adults off against one another.

- Is endlessly argumentative.
- Does not keep his word, not even when he has negotiated the conditions himself.
- Is rude *("Get lost...")*.
- Always talks back.
- Walks away in the middle of a 'conversation'
- Exploits any loopholes in the rules *("You didn't say anything about THAT!")*.

1.2.b. Reviewing the role of the adults in the problem

Do the following:
- Realise that the child's seriously inappropriate behaviour is always linked to some form of behaviour on the part of you as the adult.
- Check whether you display any of the behaviours listed below. Add to the list if necessary.
  - Although you continuously try to reason with the child, it is impossible to hold a reasonable conversation.
  - You feel you are in a no-win situation.
  - You are in a situation that you, as the parent or teacher, do not want to be in.
  - You have a tendency to keep going after the child, constantly checking whether they are sticking to their word.
  - You refuse to put up with this any longer ("Who do they think they are?").
  - You are inclined to use discipline that is too strict.
  - You feel a strong sense of anger welling up inside you.
  - You notice that sometimes you hate the child.
  - You can become enraged when you are confronted with the child's inapproachable attitude.
  - Being frustrated costs a great deal of energy but does not seem to have much effect.
  - You have a tendency to preach to the child.
  - After every new incident you ask the child, "Why"?
  - You feel angry, sad, powerless, disappointed and/or exhausted.
  - The family is divided as to the best course of action.
  - You have a tendency to withdraw and refuse to get involved at all.
  - You are tired from all the efforts you have made to strike bargains with the child, which never last.
  - You have decided that the child is going to have to sort out his own problems.
  - You have a tendency to look for explanations, for example that is simply in the child's nature.
  - You have a tendency to feel sorry for yourself ("Why me?").
  - As a teacher, you have a tendency to blame the parents, or as a parent to blame the school, and to leave it at that.
  - You are very concerned about what will happen at the next school or in the community, without the protection the child currently enjoys.
  - Your relationship with the child is caught in vicious circles.
  - In spite of all your efforts to make everything right, things always go wrong.
  - There is wedge between the parents, or between the parents and the school.
  - You do not know how to intervene, you intervene sometimes, or not at all, or you are too strict.
  - One parent thinks the other is too strict, and one thinks the other is too lenient.
  - You respond in a way that often tends to escalate the situation.

- You find yourself doing things out of anger and frustration that you later regret.
- You find that all efforts to start a conversation with the child are wasted.
- As a parent, you cling to one explanation for the child's behaviour and think that the school just does not understand.
- As a childcare worker or teacher you explain the behaviour in professional terms and think that the parents simply refuse to understand.
- You hope that the child will outgrow it ("We were all young once").
- As parents you have already heard a lot of criticism of your child, for example, from the school, clubs, neighbours or family.
- You have already concluded that well-meaning advice does not work.
- As parents you say that the child has to shape up now or leave home or the school.
- You see that letting the child experience the consequences does not help. The child does not seem to feel anything.
- You have tried different ways of working on the problem, but nothing seems to help.
- You feel paralysed by the child's behaviour.

1.2.c. Reviewing the role of the environment in the problem

Do the following:
- Keep in mind that inappropriate behaviour can drive a deep wedge between people and unleash a great deal of emotion.
- Describe situations where this is the case. Include brothers, sisters, parents, other family members, fellow students, teachers, other people at school, children and leaders at clubs and sports organisations, neighbours and others.
- Check whether you noticed any of the behaviours listed below in the environment of the child. Add to the list if necessary.
    - The school has tried to make it clear that the child's behaviour is unacceptable.
    - The school says that the child does not belong there.
    - You have noticed that the child is no longer invited to birthday parties.
    - The child is being bullied, in the street or over the internet. Other children gang up on the child.
    - Friends no longer call.
    - Some teachers are capable of dealing with the problems, but there are always conflicts with others. It is difficult to discuss the conflicts with such teachers.
    - The child has become a scapegoat.
    - Other parents complain about the child.
    - The police have been contacted about the child, and there may even be talk of a community service sentence.
    - The child is frequently sent away from the table, the classroom, sports training, a party, a club or some other group activity.
    - There is a wedge between different people or groups in the child's environment. This might involve brothers, sisters, family, friends, acquaintances, neighbours, teammates, coaches, teachers, the school principal, etc. It can be a very deep wedge, one that substantially disrupts existing relationships.
    - The family loses contact with other family members, friends and neighbours and becomes isolated.
    - Brothers and sisters say they hate the child.

Consider the following:

A child's inappropriate behaviour usually shows up in contact with others. The child makes others angry during a direct confrontation, or when others are confronted with the consequences of behaviour. The child's role in this is a failure to behave 'normally'. The child fails to stick to the bargain, despite promising to do so. He may think that he does not have to meet the "abnormal" requirements of the people around him. At the same time, the child may demand that those same people hold up their end of the bargain or meet specific requirements. The child can be very unreasonable and at the same time have a very strong sense of justice. Punishment usually just makes him angrier.

The child is an expert at finding your Achilles' heel and doing exactly what you disapprove of most. There is no reasoning with them about their behaviour. The child is not capable of reflecting on his own behaviour. This indicates that the child is not functioning at a level that is age-appropriate. It makes others very angry and brings out the worst in them. A child with behavioural problems often highlights your own weak spots. You react to this, and so the situation continues to escalate.

Your reactions and emotions as an adult also play a role in keeping the situation alive. You may have waited too long in the expectation that the child would change of his own accord. Or you may have given the child too little leeway. Your response may be too strict or not strict enough. You may continue talking in situations that call for intervention. It may be that your response is adequate but the child's behaviour is just too difficult. The bottom line is that your interactions with the child have taken a turn that leads to discouragement, powerlessness and anger. The child responds to that, and this fuels further escalations.

It is important to realise that you are a participant in this interaction because then you can start to change your role. You can use your energy to learn a systematic approach, which essentially involves responding consistently to the child's behaviour, based on a different attitude and a different way of dealing with the problem. This system is built into this behavioural programme.

Behavioural problems usually involve others besides the child and the family. People in the child's environment can also play a role. Behavioural problems can lead to a range of negative feelings and expressions between the child, family members and other people. In turn, the fear of others' disapproval can prevent you from intervening in serious behavioural problems. Other people may feel they have been tolerant for far too long. A confrontation with an angry environment can be very upsetting for the parents of a child with behavioural problems. As a result, the situation can escalate. The response of the child's environment to serious behavioural problems can be a great source of shame to the parents. Once you have reached the end of your tether, in educational terms, it is very difficult to muster a cheerful, decisive response.

It is also possible for a child with behavioural problems to function better, or even quite satisfactorily, in certain environments. Because these environments place less pressure on the child and on you, they can be useful when planning and carrying out interventions.

1.3. Ask yourself who is in charge

Portrait of a younger child

It is not easy for Jill to decide who is in charge at her house. However, consulting the checklist gets her thinking. It seems as if Josh knows that she is trying to keep the situation at home from becoming unbearable. It seems as if he uses this knowledge to do things when he is around her that he knows he should not do. If she says anything about it, he becomes even more obstinate. Sometimes she ignores things she knows are wrong. Amy notices this right away, and confronts Jill with it, saying, "Mummy, Josh is not supposed to do that."

The price of intervening has become high - sometimes too high for Jill. When she decided not let him get away with placing a bag of sweets in her trolley, Josh threw a huge tantrum in a crowded supermarket. What is she to do? It seems as if she cannot do anything right.

Portrait of an older child

Nathan's parents are all too aware of the fact that they have not been in control for several years. Nathan does exactly as he pleases. It is difficult for his parents to pinpoint when they lost control. After all, they wanted to show their child they trusted him. Last year things went badly wrong at school. During a long conversation with his father Nathan finally admitted that he had not done enough work. He said he realised he would have to shape up and promised to really do his best over the next few months, starting with the next exam week. But, of course he stayed out late on Friday and Saturday the weekend before the exams. During Sunday lunch his father could not help lecturing him. He reminded Nathan of their talk. Nathan replied, "Listen, it was what you wanted, not me!" He then yawned in his father's face and asked him if he had stopped preaching.

Use the two checklists to help you determine who is in charge.

1.3.a. Reviewing the role of the child

Do the following:
- Check whether the child displays any of the behaviours listed below. Add to the list if necessary.
  - The child always has the last word.
  - The child manages to get their own way by nagging.
  - The child wins in every "educational" situation.
  - The child uses tantrums to get their own way.
  - The child does not listen to requests, arguments or pleas, but does exactly as he pleases.
  - The child treats you like a doormat.
  - The child feels he has rights but no obligations.
  - The child intimidates you with verbal arguments and ends up getting his way.
  - The child tries to outsmart you (See page 101, Appendix A) by forcing you to stick to the rules and making you responsible. You have the feeling you are being manipulated.
  - The child objects to every request, knowing they can win the argument.
  - Somehow the child manages to avoid confrontations about their behaviour, and is clever at recognising your blind spots.

- The child always has an excuse ready to explain why he repeatedly fails to hold up his end of the bargain.
- The child places you in an impossible situation: whether you intervene or not, you are always in the wrong.

1.3.b. Reviewing the role of the adult

Do the following:

- Check whether you, as the adult, display any of the behaviours listed below. Add to the list if necessary.
  - Avoiding intervening to prevent escalations.
  - Imposing increasingly harsh punishments without results.
  - Trying to show the child who's the boss by punishing them for longer, but to no avail.
  - Constantly lecturing the child in the hope that he will see the error of his ways.
  - Constantly asking the child why he behaves in a certain way in an effort to work out what is driving the child's actions.
  - Always addressing the substance of the child's arguments.
  - Justifying the child's behaviour on the grounds that others do it as well.
  - Justifying the inappropriate behaviour on the grounds that someone else has provoked it.
  - Blaming someone else for the child's inappropriate behaviour.
  - Delaying intervention in the hope that the problem will just go away after puberty, or during the school holiday, or at some other point in the future.
  - Failing to intervene in long-standing inappropriate behaviour because "you were once young too".
  - Continuing to avoid intervening because you think someone else should do it.
  - Continuing to avoid intervening because another adult's intervention is too harsh.
  - Always thinking up new reasons to avoid intervening.
  - Threatening to intervene and then fail to follow through.
  - Being inconsistent in the way you intervene.
  - Feeling reluctant to intervene based on memories of your own childhood experiences.

Consider the following:

There is a hierarchy in any educational situation. As the adult you bring up the child, educate him and teach him about rules. You set the limits and make it possible for the child to thrive. Regardless of the style you choose, you, as the adult, should be the one taking the lead. If a child who shows inappropriate behaviour notices that the adult is not providing adequate guidance, this creates an educational vacuum. The child can take control and force you to give up your position in the hierarchy. The child will then behave as if he is on the same level as you. This sometimes leads to escalations, and the suggestion that you and the child are equals (these are called symmetrical escalations). It is a victory for the child but it does him no good, and you will feel as impotent as a beetle on its back, waving its legs in the air. It is an unsafe position for both parties.

Behavioural problems often disrupt the normal hierarchy in a family or classroom. The child behaves inappropriately and you, as the adult, may lose control of the educational situation. The opposite can also be true. Failure to maintain the normal hierarchy in the family or classroom may itself be the cause of the child's inappropriate behaviour. In both situations, the child appears to be in control of the educational situation, and does not want to give up that control. For you, the loss of control means sometimes you react too harshly, or that your interventions are no longer effective. Becoming aware of this is one the objectives of this part of the programme. Once you have this awareness you can start working on restoring a more normal hierarchy in the family or classroom. You are in charge of coaching the child to develop more appropriate behaviour.

1.4. Describe your concerns and your hopes

Portrait of a younger child

Jill does have concerns about Josh. She quickly jots down a number of things. Will he be able to make friends? Will he be banned from the football team he has just joined? Will he become the kind of boy who bullies others and is bullied? What about his relationship with his grandmother? And with her husband? Jill is also concerned about whether she and her husband can agree on a strategy. She does not enjoy thinking about these things. And right now she cannot really think of anything that gives her hope.

Portrait of an older child

Nathan's parents are aware that things are moving in entirely the wrong direction. Their greatest concern is that they are unable to do anything themselves to change this. The only hope they still have is based on the knowledge that he used to be such a nice boy. Maybe this is a just a phase he is going through and things will be all right in the end. But in order for this to happen, he first has to make it through secondary school. And at this point his grades are not very good, especially not for someone who is repeating a year. If he fails again he will have to leave school.

Nathan's father knows that preaching does not help. Nor does punishment. Nathan just laughs it off: "Hey Dad, have you read another book about it?" Nathan recently called home at four in the morning to announce that he did not have any transport. To avoid the situation degenerating into a complete disaster, his father picked him up from a club in a neighbouring town. Nathan asked if it was all right if a friend came along too. His father did not know the boy at all, and it was a silent journey. If his other son had acted in this way, he would have told him that if wanted to dance he would have to pay the piper.

We have seen how powerless the child's inappropriate behaviour can make you feel. That powerlessness has to be regarded as an unwanted educational situation.

Use the checklists below to work out what the long-term and short-term consequences of this unwanted educational situation might be.

1.4.a. Checking short-term consequences

Do the following:
- Formulate your short-term concerns about what will happen if the child's inappropriate behaviour continues. Also formulate any short-term hopes you have, using the list below, adding items if necessary. In the short term there is concern/hope about:
  - The child
  - The parents

- Other children in the family
- Other family members
- The situation at school
- Teachers/the school principal
- Classmates
- Friends
- Neighbours and neighbourhood children
- Sports clubs

1.4.b. Checking long-term consequences

Do the following:
- Formulate your long-term concerns, as an adult, about what will happen if the child's inappropriate behaviour continues. Also formulate long-term hopes you have, using the list below, adding items if necessary.
  In the long term there is concern/hope about:
  - The child
  - The parents
  - Other children in the family
  - Other family members
  - The situation at school
  - Teachers/the school principal
  - Classmates
  - Friends
  - Neighbours and neighbourhood children
  - Sports clubs

Consider the following:
Behavioural problems are often directly related to the child's future. Matters such as social development, homework, coming home late, substance abuse, being sent out of the classroom or being given a final warning by the school or a sports club can all have short-term or long-term consequences. In the case of serious behavioural problems, the consequence for the very near future is that matters come to a head. Usually this involves the removal or exclusion of the child, for example, from a holiday, school camp, sports match, visit to grandparents, church service, the December holidays, a sleepover, exam week or birthday party. If the behavioural problem is a source of great concern, *hoping* and *doing nothing* do not make for a good combination. This is something you need to be aware of. It is the first step towards converting paralysing concern into effective action. Of course you hope that problems will not arise. But when serious behavioural problems exist, it is better to assume that they will occur. Then you can prepare for them.

1.5. Determine whether the current situation can be allowed to continue

Portrait of a younger child

Having gone through the first part of this programme, Jill is convinced that things cannot continue as they are. She has the feeling that Josh is not happy with his situation. The atmosphere at home is terrible. She did not get married so that she could spend her time fighting about one of the children. She does not know what to do next, but she knows she has had enough. When she discusses this with her husband, he is not immediately convinced. He thinks that Josh simply has to learn some discipline. Jill argues that punishing him all the time will not solve the problem. But her husband is not prepared to give up that easily. He says that he will try instilling at least a few norms and values in their family. He thinks that Jill is too lenient, and as a consequence the children will never learn.

In the past this would have made Jill very angry. She would have cried that it was easy enough for her husband to say that when he was out of the house all day, and came home tired and irritable because he had had a busy day at work. He did not give Josh any latitude at all. That was the easy way out. But she does not want to fall into this all-too-familiar pattern again. Now she says to her husband, "Okay. I hear what you're saying. But I don't want to go on like this. I'm convinced that Josh is simply stepping into the gap that we leave open for him. I think we should do things differently, and I think we should do it together. We need to stop scolding him in the hope that it will help. And I need to stop avoiding intervention, in the hope that it will all blow over. It doesn't help."

Her husband is still unconvinced. He continues to say that things will all work out if he just gives Josh a good stern talking to every now and then. But Jill is also adamant. She says, "How long do we have to wait for good behaviour? And how bad does Josh's behaviour have to get before you realise that something has to be done?" Her husband sees the determined look in her eyes. He is not quite sure what to say.

Portrait of an older child

When the temperature outside has been freezing for a while, the water in a pond may still take the form of water, but if one small twig falls on the surface of the water, it will crystallise and rapidly become ice.

Something similar has happened with Nathan's parents. For several years now they have seen their son slip away from them. They can no longer get a grip on him. And when Nathan messes up during the first exam week of the school year he has had to repeat, all of the unpleasantness crystallises into a sudden decision on the part of his father. He realises that it may be too late for Nathan, but if he does not adopt a different approach to his behaviour, things will definitely take a disastrous turn. It will not be easy. Nathan will not readily give up his position at the top of the family hierarchy. But his father feels it is not right that he, his wife and the family's other two children should suffer under Nathan's tyranny. Moreover, Nathan is headed in the wrong direction, and his father wants to put a stop to this. His wife is so glad when he raises the subject that evening. She wants to know exactly what his plan is. "I don't really know, but I know that I don't want to go on like this," he responds.

The educational situation has now been mapped out. Use the three focal points below to evaluate the need for intervention. If you do not think that intervention is necessary, you should determine how long, and until what point, you want to delay intervention.

1.5.a. Drawing conclusions

| Do the following:
- Based on the situation you have mapped out, decide whether the current situation can continue to exist.
- Then decide whether intervention is necessary now, or if it can be delayed, and if so, for how long.
- If your conclusion is that the behaviour is not too bad, decide how bad it has to get before intervention is necessary.
- If you are already following this programme, indicate whether your current strategy is working, and what its strengths and weaknesses are.

1.5.b. Setting a time limit

| Do the following:
- Indicate precisely where you draw the line in terms of tolerating the inappropriate behaviour.
- Decide how long the child's behaviour has to last before intervention is necessary.
- Provide arguments that justify delaying intervention.
- If you are already following the programme, work out how long you will need, and be able, to continue this strategy.

1.5.c. Setting a limit with regard to an acceptable level of functioning

| Do the following:
- Decide where you draw the line in terms of tolerating the inappropriate behaviour.
- Decide how bad the child's behaviour has to become before intervention is necessary.
- Provide arguments that justify delaying intervention.
- If you have already completed the six steps in this programme, work out how long you will need, and be able, to continue this strategy.

|| Consider the following:
This behavioural programme assumes that there is no such thing as an educational situation in which there are no limits. Like the proverbial straw that broke the camel's back, untreated behavioural problems continue until the limit is reached. At some point, intervention is necessary. However, it is more difficult to decide when to make this decision if you are not sure whether you should intervene at all, if you think that matters are not all that serious, if you have already intervened once, without results, if others advise against intervention, or if your partner does not back you up. You might then conclude that there is no point in intervening.

Perhaps you tend to avoid doing anything about the inappropriate behaviour. What you really want is for the behaviour to go away by itself. You are willing to wait for this to happen. It started for no apparent reason, so why shouldn't it simply disappear of its own accord? Perhaps you have convinced yourself that it will go away after puberty. You may also think that the inappropriate behaviour is down to circumstances beyond your control. If only the school would just change, or other parents would be more understanding, or society were different, things would be better.

You need to understand that this kind of behaviour will not simply go away. As the adult you may well have your doubts about the need to intervene. But in that case you need to ask yourself how long the inappropriate behaviour has to continue before intervention becomes necessary. How long do you want to continue in this way? You also have to ask yourself how bad the child's behaviour has to become to justify intervention. There is a limit to what can be termed acceptable behaviour. Ask yourself, "Is this what I want?"

If in doubt, you can take an active stance. You can indicate different moments in time when you will ask a third party about the relevant behaviour. As parents, you can stay in touch with the school or your child's sports coach. Clearly, it is not easy to discuss behavioural problems. They are accompanied by rejection and shame. However, regularly asking about your child's behaviour at school, during sports activities and even in the neighbourhood provides a basis for discussion. And discussion is a form of cooperation that can help you determine whether intervention is necessary. Healthy doubt does not have to lead to avoidance.

Placing limitations on inappropriate behaviour is not simply a question of skill. It is also culturally determined, by, among other things, micro-cultures such as the family, school and other groups. This means that you, as an adult, may have to deal with limitations placed on the child's behaviour by others outside of your own micro-culture. Although you may have a different opinion, you might be confronted with limitations imposed by the neighbours, school, sports club or authorities. Even if you think that the response of third parties is disproportionate, it is a good idea to take the limits of other people's flexibility into account. The questions remain the same: how bad does the child's behaviour have to be before intervention becomes necessary, and how long can it be allowed to go on?

When determining whether the current situation can be allowed to continue, you should consider not only the child's behaviour but also the child's environment. What does the environment contribute to the behaviour? If you focus only on the fact that the child kicks other children in the playground, you will overlook the fact that this usually follows severe bullying by another child. You may also show strong disapproval of the child's behaviour without realising that you, as the adult, continually give them the opportunity to misbehave.

The purpose of this chapter was to help you take stock of the child's inappropriate behaviour, and to give you some idea of the seriousness of the situation. And to encourage you to ask yourself whether the seriousness and duration of the situation are such that it is time to intervene.

In the second chapter we assume that intervention is necessary. However, as the adult you cannot simply adopt a different approach without being aware of your current approach. The situation in which you find yourself makes you feel discouraged, powerless and angry. That is why chapter 2 addresses your own attitude towards work. In chapter 3 we will go on to plan an intervention.

2. Fix your own attitude first

2. FIX YOUR OWN ATTITUDE FIRST

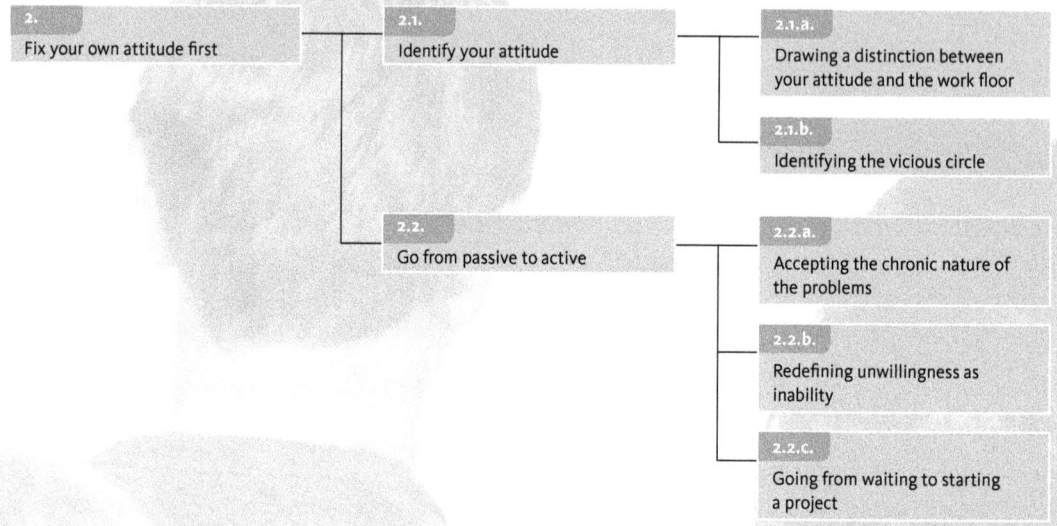

2. Fix your own attitude first
- **2.1.** Identify your attitude
  - **2.1.a.** Drawing a distinction between your attitude and the work floor
  - **2.1.b.** Identifying the vicious circle
- **2.2.** Go from passive to active
  - **2.2.a.** Accepting the chronic nature of the problems
  - **2.2.b.** Redefining unwillingness as inability
  - **2.2.c.** Going from waiting to starting a project

What is this chapter about?

You have tried everything and nothing works. Your mood swings from very angry to resigned, and you are unable to find an approach that really works.
This chapter helps you to break out of this impasse.

2. Fix your own attitude first

Portrait of a younger child
"You see, you can do it!"

Stephen is an experienced teacher, and over the years he has seen many changes in the education system. He has his own ideas about how today's children are being educated. He realises that he cannot change the world. But he can give the children in his year 5 class something useful. Stephen has a gift for making history come alive, and the children love his stories. Except Kyle. For Stephen, Kyle is a prime example of how not to raise your children. Kyle's behaviour is disruptive during lessons and during breaks. It's always something. Stephen has had to punish Kyle several times. Things improve then, but only for a few days. Kyle does not like to be told what to do and Stephen is unable to persuade him that he is his own worst enemy.

When Kyle disrupts a story, Stephen becomes very angry. He decides it is time for Kyle to pay the consequences. Stephen sends him out of the classroom and says he is banned from the next two storytelling sessions. Kyle spends the next two sessions in the school's central hall, working on a special assignment. During the next storytelling session he is quiet and obedient. Stephen calls him up to his desk at the end of afternoon, and gives Kyle a little speech. Stephen says: "You see, you can do it, if you just try." He also says: "And the next time I want you to stop and think before you disrupt the class…" Stephen is satisfied with his approach. He thinks that Kyle has learned his lesson. Kyle says nothing.

Portrait of an older child
"Get out of bed on time?"

James is a teenager. He finds it difficult to get up on time and get ready for school. He already has two alarm clocks next to his bed, but he sleeps through both of them. Or he turns them off and goes back to sleep. He often misses the first few hours of school. His parents are becoming desperate. They know that his grades are suffering. But they do not think it is a good idea to drag him out of bed every morning. His father has already tried that and the results were disastrous.

His mother has a plan. She will knock on James's door ten minutes after the second alarm goes off, and tell him it is time to get up but say nothing more. This works a few times, but soon knocking does not help either. James turns over and goes back to sleep. When James's mother says that she expects him to cooperate with the plan, he says he doesn't want to talk about it. Why is she making such a big thing out of it? It's his life, isn't it? And anyway, last week she was late herself and didn't knock on the door until it was too late to go to school.

Introduction

This chapter deals with your own attitude. You will understand the text better if you first read the metaphor about the orchard on page 111, Appendix C. You will learn in this chapter how to base your educational interventions on an active attitude. Becoming aware of how disappointment has made your own attitude passive is part of this process. As is fixing your attitude. The objective of fixing your attitude is to help you make a clearer distinction between the child and his behaviour. When children have serious behavioural problems, this distinction quickly becomes muddled. The child and the undesirable behaviour become one and the same. And that makes it difficult for you as an adult to give an adequate response without getting angry. Fixing your attitude is actually about fixing your interaction with the child.

Undesirable behaviour leads to a vicious circle in which the child is unwilling to cooperate and you, the adult, feel powerless. This applies to parents, teachers and childcare workers. The powerlessness of your approach feeds the child's unwillingness to display more acceptable behaviour. And the child's unwillingness reinforces your own powerlessness. You can hope that the undesirable behaviour will go away in time. That usually does not happen. You can also look for recipes that tell you how to deal with the behaviour. However, using standard education tactics will not eliminate the feeling of powerlessness.

You as the adult have lost your grip on the child's behaviour. You feel that the child is in charge. You have tried everything, but this has produced nothing but frustration. Or you were desperately hoping that the behaviour would just go away and are now forced to face reality. If your child's behaviour is seriously disruptive, you may end up being deeply depressed, with very little confidence in your capabilities. This has a major impact on your attitude, and your attitude determines how you approach the problem. You may end up seeing everything in terms of black and white. Black represents overreaction. White represents an inadequate response. Both "choices" lead to further powerlessness, which undermines your attitude. You can't do anything right! You have already had so much advice and so many tips that did not work in the end. Do they really think their advice will work? No one understands how difficult this is for you!

You may be angry with childcare workers or school representatives who have so far provided little real support. Or who have simply expressed their disapproval. All of this makes you feel that you are in a hopeless situation. Disappointment and exhaustion are now the basis of your attitude, and that is the starting point of this programme. Once you are in that hopeless situation, one more piece of advice is not likely to be heeded, let alone prove successful. It is therefore important to start by working on your own powerlessness and anger. Then you can use the new attitude as a basis for tackling the problem.

If you want to know how to fix your attitude, it is important to identify your current attitude. The following focus points can make you aware of your own attitude. Work on your own attitude before starting the intervention. Keep in mind that this can be a long, drawn out process.

2.1. Identify your attitude

Portrait of a younger child

Stephen wants the best for the children in his class. He gives them more than just the standard curriculum. His own background has encouraged him to see teaching norms and values as part of his responsibility. But he has trouble understanding Kyle and his behavioural problems. Kyle does exactly what they have agreed he would not do. And for Stephen, honouring an agreement is important. So Kyle does not meet the norm that Stephen applies.

At first Stephen tries to deal with Kyle's disruptive behaviour in the routine manner. He has had children like this in the classroom before. He knows that what they need is a good dressing down. Then the behaviour will stop. But Kyle is different. Kyle has found Stephen's Achilles' heel, by disrupting his storytelling sessions. That makes Stephen very angry. He increases the punishment and gives him an even stronger dressing down. Stephen thinks that imposing his own norms will change Kyle's behaviour.

Because Kyle is silent throughout the dressing down, Stephen thinks he has solved the problem, but his solution centres around his own convictions. It does not focus specifically on Kyle's limited capabilities, and is therefore not an effective way of dealing with behavioural problems. The teacher's attitude is normative. By imposing and promoting his own norms he is choosing a content-based approach. That can work with children who function at a higher level. But Kyle does not function at that level; the content-based approach means that he is being addressed at a level that is too high for him. The information goes in one ear and out the other, and Kyle learns nothing from it. However, he has learned to say nothing when the teacher is lecturing him.

The teacher's attitude is also passive. He lays down the law once more and expects the disruptive behaviour to stop. Then Stephen can get back to doing what he thinks is right, what he is good at: teaching and telling stories. Stephen is assuming that Kyle functions at an age-appropriate level, and that he is therefore simply unwilling to cooperate. His assumptions are not based on Kyle's actual level of functioning, a level at which he is in fact incapable of displaying more appropriate behaviour. When things go badly, it is the child's fault. When things go well, everything is normal, and that is down to the teacher.

In this portrait we see that Stephen's skills as a teacher are reflected in the transfer of norms and values to the children in his class. And in his ability to inspire children with his stories. However, these very skills make him vulnerable in his dealings with a child with behavioural problems. He can no longer get by on the strength of these skills. The teacher thinks he is addressing the problem, but he is actually passive. He is caught in a mental pattern that is black and white, and he chooses primarily black. He thinks this is for the good of the child, but Stephen's actions are not based on the level at which the child actually functions. His approach is well-intentioned, but not yet professional. It costs the teacher extra energy, but yields little. It simply feeds existing ideas.

This gradually creates a vicious circle, which can trap even an experienced teacher. It is the vicious circle of disappointment, anger, and powerlessness that often accompanies serious behavioural problems.

Portrait of an older child

A clear problem has arisen: James has been threatened with suspension, which could cost him a whole year of school. But it seems as if only his parents are aware of this. They cannot convince James of the necessity of getting up on time. The parents have landed in a black and white position. His father has tried the physical approach to getting James out of bed. Is that so wrong? (black) James's mother now has a plan of her own for solving the problem. It is a friendly, but ineffective plan. She tries to find a solution that will get James to school on time. But James has no incentive to show any involvement. His mother does her best by proposing more content-based solutions. She hopes that James will listen to reason. But that does not happen. The situation slips from her grasp.

And so his mother is now also in a powerless position (white). She is in a bind. If she does not wake him he will not get to school on time. If she does wake James, he still goes back to sleep. A vicious circle is created, in which the father accuses the mother of cosseting James. The mother tries not to make the father angry because that is not helpful. She tries to think of some way of persuading James to get to school on time. And James? He thinks his father is an old fogey. And his mother is not a worthy opponent. He turns over and goes back to sleep.

James's parents are actually very angry. He lies around in bed like a lazy prince while they worry about his school performance. All they get is a sneer if they try to help him. Moreover, they fight with one another about it. The fear that he will be suspended and have to repeat a year prompts them to do things James should be doing. How did this happen?

After every new solution, both parents hope that James will mend his ways. But the opposite is true. He seems to be turning away from his parents even more, and refusing to accept that it is his problem at all. And every day his parents are disappointed to discover that James is still asleep. They are starting to run out of "solutions". What else can they think of to get him out of bed on time?

The focus points below can help you to become more aware of your attitude and to identify a vicious circle.

2.1.a. Drawing a distinction between your attitude and the work floor

Do the following:
- Realise that the way in which you do or do not intervene on the shop floor is determined by your attitude. Your attitude is the product of your own experience with intervention. It may be an experience with this child or with another one. But it may also be related to your own memories or convictions.
- Use the following checklist to help you distinguish between your work attitude and the shop floor:
  - Identify your real opinion of this behaviour.
  - Identify what you think needs to happen, and who needs to do it.
  - Think about whether this conviction is what determines your approach on the shop floor.
  - Think about whether your actions on the shop floor are the result of powerlessness, discouragement, disappointment or anger. Is it useful to maintain this attitude?
  - Think about whether your attitude has changed since a previous round of this programme. Have you slipped back into powerlessness?
  - Do you have the feeling that your attitude has a positive impact on your approach? Is it useful to maintain this attitude?

2.1.b. Identifying the vicious circle

Do the following:
- Check if a vicious circle has been created: does the inappropriate behaviour continue regardless of whether or not you intervene?
- Use the following checklist, adding points if necessary.
  - Based on your convictions you have intervened decisively, but the behaviour just seems to get worse.
  - You are constantly angry: you feel powerless, disappointed and exhausted by the child's behaviour.
  - You always hope for improvement, but your hopes are dashed again and again. You clearly do not have a deal with the child, even though you think you do.
  - You are in an impossible position: saying yes is wrong but so is saying no.
  - You think you have a solid agreement with the child, but the child repeatedly violates the agreement.

- Something has happened that paralyzes your ability to act in the educational situation
- You have the feeling that no matter what you do, the child will not comply with your wishes.
- For every educational decision taken, one adult thinks they are too lenient while the other thinks they are too strict.
- In the school situation, there are parents who blame the school, a school who blames the parents, and a child who is constantly being disciplined.

Consider the following

As an adult you often feel a great need for practical advice. You have however noticed that much of the advice does not cover the entire situation, or does not cover it at all. You have already learned that advice from third parties such as "Chin up" or "It will all work out in the end" are unhelpful and irritating. Comments such as these do not do justice to the complexity and intransigence of the educational problem. But the same is true of comments such as "We only want practical advice" from the adults dealing with children who have serious behavioural problems. There is no standard advice for dealing with complex situations.

The question now is how can an adult get out of a difficult educational position. How can he or she get a grip on the situation? Clearly, this is not an easy matter. You are often already at the end of your rope, exhausted from looking for solutions. Inappropriate behaviour confronts you again and again with what you cannot accept. A child who does not keep promises, who always whines, who always asks for more without giving anything in return, makes you angry. Your own norms and values are being stomped on. The child always knows just how to find your Achilles' heel. You are also ashamed of the behaviour and of what others might say about it. That is why you think it has to stop RIGHT NOW. And if that does not happen, you become even angrier. You feel you are caught in a vicious circle.

A vicious circle is created when an adult does something – or does not do it – in the hope of decreasing the inappropriate behaviour, while in fact the behaviour continues and may be getting worse. You have noticed that both acting and failing to act have the same effect. This can easily lead to an escalation of the conflict with the child.

For example, harsh discipline makes the child even more difficult to reach and the child withdraws. The adult responds with even harsher measures. The child has to realise how serious the matter is! However, the result is that the child becomes even more difficult to approach. Sooner or later, this spiral leads to an explosion. The opposite may also occur. In some cases every action on the part of the child results in the adult becoming more uninvolved. This leads to more action by the child. The child whines until his pocket money is increased. The parent becomes increasingly irritated with the whining, but eventually gives in. The child gets his way by whining, and the parents give in to stop the whining. The child now knows exactly what to do to get his own way: whine.

This is how inappropriate behaviour sucks you into a dark hole and paralyzes you. It puts you in a hopeless position. No matter what you do or say, the inappropriate behaviour continues. You are left feeling helpless and angry; you continue unsuccessfully tackling the problem or you avoid confrontation whenever possible. Your attitude has become passive.

A passive attitude is one characterised by a black and white mentality. The colour **black** represents an attitude based on anger and adherence to a rigid, unattainable norm. You are convinced that harsher punishments will work. You hope that fierce opposition to the behaviour will rid you of the burden. In the face of this, the child may become highly indifferent to punishment, and secretly try to satisfy his needs some other way. This only increases the burden on you, the adult.

The colour **white** represents the feeling that you have no grip on the things that happen to you. You are convinced that intervention is pointless because it does not help anyway. You become an expert at avoiding confrontation in the hope that it will lessen your load. The child is then in a position to use your avoidance to strengthen his own tyrannical position of power in the educational situation. This too only increases your burden.

An adult may swing back and forth between the black and white positions. That costs a great deal of energy and does not lead to effective interventions. A passive attitude leads to exhaustion. That is why it is essential to be aware of your attitude. And of your own part in fuelling an escalation of the situation. You will often notice that you have a passive attitude even though you feel you are making a huge effort.

One parent often takes the black role while the other takes the white. One parent thinks the other is much too strict, and often yields a little to the child. One parent thinks the other one is too lenient, and does not hesitate to say so. Each parent thinks the other is fuelling the escalation of the behavioural problem. Parenting, and even the relationship itself can come under considerable pressure. Here too, a passive attitude leads to exhaustion.

Before starting an intervention, you have to repair your own attitude. Your attitude is not the same as the way in which you deal with the inappropriate behaviour on the shop floor. It is important to recognise the difference. Attitude is more important than strategy, and attitude is determined by how you view the relevant behavioural problems. A particular attitude is always the starting point for dealing with behaviour. If you fail to examine your attitude, the effectiveness of your actions is inevitably limited. And for a child who has serious behavioural problems, this means trouble.

It may seem almost impossible to invest in a new approach. Fixing your attitude requires too much energy! However, experience with this programme has shown that failing to fix your attitude requires even more energy.

The next section discusses how to fix your attitude

2.2. Go from passive to active

Portrait of a younger child

Stephen uses the orchard metaphor (See page 111, Appendix C) to become more aware of the effect Kyle has on him. It is not what he had expected after a long career in education. It is as if the child is confronting him with his own blind spots. It has given him something to think about. But first there is work to do!

Stephen realises that he has had quite a few "good talks" with Kyle. They only help for a short time. The effect of punishment is also temporary. Kyle quiets down for awhile, but the same behaviour crops up a little later. He has to admit that each time he thought Kyle had understood that his behaviour was unacceptable. Apparently that is not the case; it doesn't work that way. It seems as if Kyle does not understand that he is disrupting the lesson and the storytelling session. As if he were much younger than 10 years old. Stephen understands that he has to speak to Kyle as if he were a much younger child. That he needs to be retrained, almost as if he were a toddler. This realisation prompts Stephen to ask himself: "Can I do that in the classroom? Wouldn't it be better to call in a behavioural therapist? I have 22 other children in the class." On the other hand, the current situation also causes considerable frustration and therefore uses up a lot energy.

Stephen decides to give it a try. He makes an appointment with the school's counsellor. They decide to make it their project to take a different approach to Kyle's behaviour. They will make a list of Kyle's inappropriate behaviour, and each time they will choose something to work on. It will be a kind of training. Training for a child who in some areas functions at a much younger level. The counsellor calls the parents for an appointment. Stephen realises that he is not dreading Kyle's disruptions as much as before. In fact, he is curious about how things will go.

Portrait of an older child

James's parents consult a counsellor who uses the orchard metaphor (See page 111, Appendix C) to explain their position. They immediately recognise the situation, but it takes some getting used to. They really just came for a few tips. Maybe they have overlooked something and the counsellor is sure to have some useful advice. But the counsellor starts by saying that this is seriously inappropriate behaviour, and there is no standard advice for dealing with it. The difference between attitude and the shop floor is explained to them. The counsellor says that suggestions will serve no purpose unless they can fix their own attitudes. James's father has little use for counsellors, and he is sceptical about the phrase "fixing your own attitude". However the orchard metaphor makes it clearer to him, and James's father sees that both the black and white position are expressions of a passive attitude.

The counsellor asks them if they think James will continue to be late for school, or if the problem has been solved. Both parents are convinced that he will still often be late. "Good", says the counsellor, "at least we know that now. Our real opponent is the fact that James will continue to be late." He suggests starting with that assumption. He says: "So whatever you do, accept that the inappropriate behaviour will repeat itself. This is a long-term project, which means that you should not be fixated on achieving short-term results." The father is the first to understand the implications. He says that this means that James will have to repeat a year. The counsellor says: "Yes, that may well be. But that would also be the case if you let the problem escalate by continuing to drag him out of bed every morning." He says that he does not know whether James will pass this year. In any case, the parents can take a slightly more relaxed approach to the behavioural problem. This gives the parents a somewhat liberated feeling, even though they are not happy about the prospect of James losing a year.

The counsellor concludes that the insoluble problem of James is driving a wedge between them, and explains that the black and white pattern is common to such situations. It is important to recognise that James's inappropriate behaviour is damaging their relationship. If they find themselves in a similar black and white position later in the programme, then something is wrong with the way the programme has been carried out. It is best to start again from the beginning by mapping out the situation.

The counsellor again mentions the parents' awareness of the chance of a recurrence. They confirm that this makes it possible for them to distance themselves a little from James's behavioural problem. Then the counsellor discusses the insolent, intentional, unwilling nature of the behaviour. Both parents recognise that it is James's indifferent and unapproachable attitude that makes them so angry. Then the counsellor asks them if it would be easier to distance themselves if they could see the unwillingness as an inability. "You could think of James's insolence as an indication that he functions at a much lower level for his age. As if he is incapable of functioning at his age level in this respect." This is difficult for the parents. James's mother notes that in all other respects he wants to be treated like someone his age. They would be in real trouble if they treated him like a younger child. The counsellor agrees. Teenagers and adolescents with behavioural problems want to be treated with the respect they often fail to show others.

He explains that this is one of the most effective parts of the programme; the child does not lose face because he is treated with respect. But the treatment he receives has to be absolutely consistent with the level at which he functions. So if fifteen-year old James displays behaviour that it is more consistent with that of a five-year old, the programme will start at that level. We assume that James will not like it. And we expect that it will be in his interest to try to avoid the consequences of that low level of functioning.

James's father is now better able to answer the question about distance. "It's about accepting the long-term nature of the problem. But also about seeing the angry, silly behaviour as the behaviour of a much younger child." He realises that this sheds a different light on James's behaviour. As if he can see him better from a distance. He also realises that it is useless to argue with a child who in some respects functions at such a low level. This is completely different to their earlier approach, the one that caused so much frustration. James's father takes it one step further and says, "I understand now that at that lower level you can only work on very small things. It is a bit like football training. Trainers teach their players new things on a step-by-step basis." "Yes," says the counsellor, "and that is what I mean by fixing your own attitude. You are a bit like the trainer of a young team, learning as you go what works and what doesn't. If you focus on the training, you no longer have to stand helplessly on the sidelines hoping that you win the game."

The sequence of the transition from passive to active is as follows: accept the chronic nature of the behaviour, redefine the child's unwillingness as inability, identify the actual level at which the child functions and start the behavioural programme there.

The three focus points listed below can help you make the transition from passive to active.

2.2.a. Accepting the chronic nature of the problems

Do the following:
- Be prepared for the recurrence of the behaviour. You can hope that the behaviour will not be repeated, but you assume it will.
- Be aware of the need to have a plan of action if the behaviour recurs.
- Remind yourself that this is a long-term project, so that the inappropriate behaviour does not take you by surprise every time. This will help you take a more active position.
- Be aware of what the chronic nature of the complaint means for your attitude. Use the following checklist.

- You wish that the behaviour would stop, preferably that it had already stopped yesterday.
- This behaviour, or some other inappropriate behaviour, keeps recurring. It takes you by surprise every time.
- The recurring behaviour makes you feel overwhelmed because you do not know how to deal with it.
- The chronic nature of the behavioural complaint can result in a passive attitude on the part of you, the adult.
- Passiveness cannot solve the behavioural problem.
- Both the recurrence of the inappropriate behaviour and the approach to the problem contribute to the chronic nature of the problem.
- You can expect recurrence of the inappropriate behaviour.
- It is better to expend less energy on hoping that this will not happen.
- It is better to expend less energy on disappointment when it happens anyway.
- Accepting the chronic nature of the inappropriate behaviour is the first step towards a less passive approach.

2.2.b. Redefining unwillingness as inability

Do the following:
- Read the orchard metaphor on page 111, Appendix C.
- Be aware of the need to find another way of seeing and thinking about the behavioural problem. Use the following checklist.
  - New confrontations or new efforts to avoid setting boundaries are not moves that should be repeated. It is time for a new approach.
  - Your approach tends to be based on how things should be instead of how they actually are.
  - This means that you are addressing the child at the wrong level; "normal behaviour" is a product the child is apparently not able to deliver.
  - The behaviour that makes you angry should be seen as an expression of the child's inability to behave differently.
  - The suspicion of unwillingness makes you angrier than the realisation that the child is incapable of acting differently.
  - Redefining unwillingness as inability makes it somewhat easier for you to distance yourself from the child's behaviour.
  - The child is at times better able to act appropriately than at others; he functions at different levels.
  - It is useful to avoid emphasising the unwillingness by learning to see the behaviour as inability.
  - The inability is an expression of the child's functioning at a level below his actual age.
  - An active attitude means finding the level at which the child actually functions.
  - Realise that the act of determining the child's level of functioning will in itself lead to greater professional distance.
  - Realise that a greater professional distance requires less energy than repeated disappointment, anger, hope and frustration.
  - Realise that a new way of thinking can give better insight into which interventions are possible than the same tired old way of thinking.

2.2.c. Going from waiting to starting a project

Do the following:
- Decide whether you want to make a project of breaking down the problem now, or prefer to wait awhile.
- Take the following five steps to fix your attitude:
    1. Be aware of your "lost" position (black and white in the orchard metaphor) and of the part your attitude plays in maintaining the vicious circle.
    2. Recognise the chronic nature of the behavioural problem.
    3. See the child's behaviour as inability, as an indication of a low level of functioning.
    4. Select parts of the inappropriate behaviour (See the football metaphor on page 112, Appendix C) and view dealing with them as a project. Realise that partial goals are easier to achieve.
    5. Follow the shop floor methods described in chapters 4, 5 and 6.

Consider the following:
A child with a serious behavioural problem seems to be doing everything deliberately. The child is disobedient, a bully, intent on undermining authority, and does exactly as he pleases. If you try to approach, scold or help the child, or try to make a deal, you are met with obstinacy. The child does exactly what he has agreed not to do. Or the child does not do what he agreed to do. There is no deal, even though you think you have one.

A child with a serious behavioural problem knows exactly what your Achilles' heel is, your vulnerable spot. Even if the behavioural problem is part of a condition the child suffers, it is difficult to see it as anything other than unwillingness and premeditation. And sooner or later that will make you very angry. The anger causes you to react in black and white way (See the orchard metaphor on page 111, Appendix C). You let yourself be drawn into a confrontation, or avoid setting boundaries at all. In turn, both reactions provoke more inappropriate behaviour. This is the starting point of the vicious circle, and it leads to you feeling helpless and exhausted.

Doing something about your own attitude is not the easiest route to take. Doing nothing is more comfortable. Then you can limit yourself to giving an explanation of the inappropriate behaviour, usually one based on your own background and education. The easiest explanation is: "It's in the child's nature". However, this form of procrastination immediately brands the child as a lost cause. Saying that it is in the child's nature actually means that there is nothing you can do about it. You may then feel this relieves you of the obligation to change your attitude. And that is remarkable, because if a child had Down's syndrome or another handicap, we would do everything we could to actively include him.

If we are convinced that a passive attitude is wrong, it follows that we need to adopt an active attitude. But exactly what is an active attitude? And how can it be achieved in such difficult circumstances? An active attitude involves introducing a certain amount of "professional" distance and planning and carrying out projects that are based on the current level at which the child functions. An active attitude can be achieved in a few steps. Read the metaphor about "the orchard" (page 111, Appendix C) and "taking your autistic child to a street party" (page 112, Appendix C).

Repairing your attitude involves three steps.

The **first step** is to accept the reality of the situation. Then you no longer have to waste your energy hoping that the problem will just go away. Or becoming angry if once again your expectations are not met. Or being sad and asking yourself why this is happening to you. Or worrying about how others will react. Or demanding reparation from people you think have wronged you. You realise that the behavioural problem is an opponent that you can no longer ignore, order around or wish away. Accepting its chronic nature gives you the opportunity to take a calmer look at your opponent. This creates some distance, and helps you accept the fact that dealing with this behavioural problem is going to take time. Understanding the chronic nature of the behavioural problem also helps you realise that it is pointless to hope that the problem will simply go away. Eventually this leads to a more professional approach to the behavioural problem on the shop floor. It is part of the process of taking back control over the educational situation.

The realisation and acceptance of the chronic nature of the problem can lead to a number of responses. The first may be a feeling of mourning when you realise that your approach has apparently failed. You realise how tired all those useless interventions have made you. You feel as if your suspicion that the child will never amount to anything has been confirmed. You were always afraid of this, and this realisation is saddening and difficult to accept. Accepting the chronic nature of the problem may result in a feeling of relief. Relief at the recognition that this is a serious problem that cannot be solved instantly. You are relieved of the impossible obligation to find a solution NOW, even though the conflict is sometimes acute.

The **second step** is to accept that the behaviour that makes you angry is an expression of the child's inability to behave differently. The inability reflects the fact that the child is functioning at a level below its age. The child is acting is if he were much younger because he cannot do otherwise. If you redefine unwillingness as inability, you will be less angry. The passive side of your attitude is reflected in your refusal to let go of the assumption that the child should be functioning at a more age-appropriate level. Constantly asking more than the child is capable of delivering dooms every project you start to failure.

The **third step** is to plan and carry out small projects that are geared to the child's capabilities. The active side of your attitude is reflected in your willingness to approach the child at his own functioning level. Then you can start projects with limited objectives and clear boundaries. That gives both you and the child a better overall view.

It is good to realise that training your child means that you are also in training. You are training your attitude and your technique. In other words, you are training your own educational professionalism. You can take your time with this. Do not be too hard on yourself if it does not work right away or if you let things slip a bit. Professionalism develops gradually. After a time you will notice that you respond to inappropriate behaviour with less anger and helplessness, and you are less frustrated by other inappropriate behaviour because you know it will be dealt with in turn. The child quickly catches on. We know from experience that while you are practicing on one type of behaviour, other inappropriate behaviours sometimes also decrease a little, even if you have not practiced. What the child is picking up on is primarily the change in your attitude. Changing your attitude from passive to active is not a guarantee of success but it is the key to it.

Practicing helps you to escape the vicious circle in which everything you do is wrong. Little by little, it gradually helps you replace helplessness with a new perspective. You take the initiative and are in control. You have a better idea of what is feasible, and practicing with the child becomes productive.

The opposite is also true. Your view of what is possible can disappear if you are not able to practice with the child. Parents can maintain the vicious circle if they are not consistent and do not work together. If the behavioural problem continues it may be a reflection of underlying organisational or relationship problems. At schools and in other groups as well, an inadequate response to behavioural problems may be a reflection of unsolved organisational problems. In both cases, the child with behavioural problems is an easy target for everyone else's anger.

This chapter raised your awareness of the need to fix your attitude. Now it is possible to plan an intervention from an active position. The next chapter takes us into the design studio for an explanation of the system used to plan an intervention.

3. Prepare the intervention

3. PREPARE THE INTERVENTION

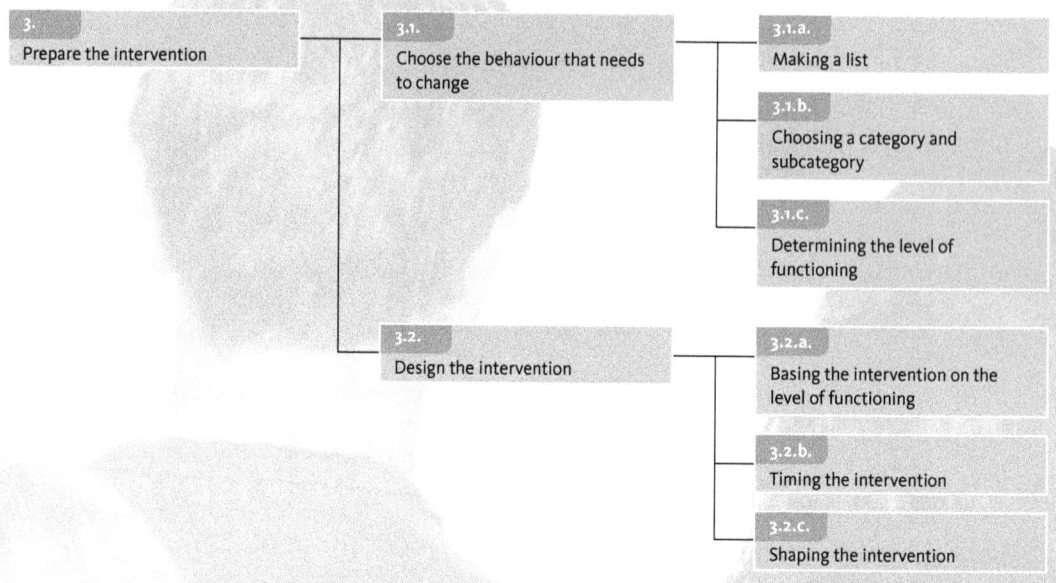

What is this chapter about?

A child's repeated inappropriate behaviour needs to be taken seriously. You cannot wait until the behaviour occurs to think of a strategy. Once you have adopted a different attitude you can learn and practice a systematic approach. This enables you to prepare targeted interventions for different situations. This chapter helps you to prepare the intervention.

3. Prepare the intervention

Portrait of a younger child
"That's not what you said!"
Luke is nine years old. He constantly teases his eleven-year old sister Jessica. She's a bit too chubby and is just entering puberty. Luke is highly adept at exploiting her insecurity. At home and at school he calls her "Miss Piggy", and makes snorting noises when she is eating. But he also kicks her under the table, and frequently hits her or pulls her pony tail. "Pigs can't feel anything anyway!" When he is handing out snacks at a birthday party, he skips her and says that it's not for pigs. He sneaks into her room and goes through her things. Luke never misses an opportunity to make his sister's life difficult.

Portrait of an older child
"Everyone else is allowed to stay out later"
Hannah is a pleasant sixteen-year old girl. She is an average student at her secondary school, and has a fairly good idea of what she wants to do when she finishes school. Since her fifteenth birthday she has been allowed to go out on Fridays and Saturdays. Her parents want her to be home by three in the morning. She also has sports and they do not want her to spend the rest of the weekend lying in bed. The problem is that Hannah never comes home on time. She often comes home at half past four and sometimes even later. First she tried to sneak in without waking them, but now that they are expecting it, she can no longer creep upstairs unnoticed.

Introduction

Everyone experiences problems with a child or adolescent at some point. If you ask other adults for advice they will tell you what worked for them. Or they give advice based on personal convictions about behavioural problems. Sometimes that works, but often it does not. The same advice cannot be applied on a one-to-one basis to other children with behavioural problems. Standard methods work almost exclusively in a particular context. And serious behavioural problems are usually too complex to be dealt with by means of standard methods. You would have to memorise a whole battery of standard methods in order not to be left at a loss for words when a problem arises.

That is why this programme is not based on standard solutions. It does provide a fixed system for devising interventions. The system results in different interventions for different situations, but the system itself is always the same. And that means that you can practice using it to deal with different situations.

You learn that it is not possible to practice on all different kinds of behaviour at the same time. The system is designed to be practiced in small doses. This makes the project achievable for the child, but also for you as trainer. Practicing in small doses teaches the adult to use the programme's system. You train yourself to train the child. And as a result it gradually becomes possible for you to deal with other behavioural situations faster and more effectively.

Each time you will choose one item to work on from your list of inappropriate behaviours. Remember, you cannot practice two things at once. This implies that while you are training one type of inappropriate behaviour, others will continue as before. You might continue to respond to these other inappropriate behaviours in the old way. But something will have changed. You are no longer in a paralysed, powerless situation. You will begin to feel more confident about your approach to the other inappropriate behaviours, knowing that their turn is also coming. Practicing strengthens your own work attitude. The child often notices the change. Training a limited number of behavioural aspects frequently results in an improvement in the rest of the child's behaviour. This is called generalisation. However, sometimes the child's behavioural problem is very persistent. That is still unpleasant, but if it no longer makes you feel paralysed and powerless, you will be able to take better, clearer follow-up measures.

Be very specific in your preparations about defining the inappropriate behaviour. A vague description makes the behaviour untrainable. Simply telling the child "he should just stop shouting all the time" is less effective than if the child knows exactly what will happen if he does not stop shouting fifteen seconds after the adult has raised a warning finger.

Mapping out the situation, repairing your own work attitude and preparing the intervention all take place before involving the child in the process. It is a project, and you need to be well-prepared. Compare it to a mountain hike: make sure you are well-prepared, do not walk too far if you are untrained, and be prepared for disappointments. But above all remember that the more accustomed you become to walking at this altitude, the easier it will be to complete the hike.

3.1. Choose the behaviour that needs to change

Portrait of a younger child

Things are getting out of hand with Luke, and his parents realise they need to intervene. They each make a list of Luke's inappropriate behaviour toward his sister. They are shocked by how easy it is to list more than ten items. They notice that Luke requires no provocation to tease Jessica. It happens during meals, but also in the bathroom, during family outings, and after school. Actually, given the chance, Luke will tease her all day. When the parents compare their lists, they see that some areas overlap, but there are also behaviours that one of the two had forgotten. They can now divide the behaviours on the list into a few categories. They choose physical bullying, verbal teasing, and not respecting Jessica's privacy.

As subcategories of physical bullying they list: hitting, kicking, hair pulling, tripping. For verbal teasing they list: nasty remarks about her weight, making pig noises and swearing at her. Failure to respect the privacy of Jessica's room and her things is both a category and subcategory. They want Luke to stop going into her room whenever he likes and taking things or breaking them. They have studied the football metaphor and so they know that they cannot practice all football techniques at once. They choose a simple subject for their first intervention: hair pulling. Both parents want this to stop immediately. They have already spoken to Luke about it. Once or twice the father has even tried pulling Luke's own hair when he caught him doing this. Luke was outraged and he called his father a child abuser. An attempt to explain this and talk about it was disrupted by loud crying on Luke's part. Luke behaved for a few days but after that he could not resist pulling Jessica's hair again.

Luke's parents believe he functions at a low level in this respect. They realise that at this point it is useless to continue talking or awarding stickers for good behaviour. They find it difficult to understand why Luke does this. But they know it is time for it to stop.

Portrait of an older child

Hannah's parents have stopped objecting when she comes home late. She has usually been drinking and that does not help the conversation. If they bring it up later, Hannah is recalcitrant. She doesn't want to talk about it. She accuses her parents of nagging. And anyway, "everyone else" has a later curfew. She is the laughing stock of her entire circle of friends! Arguing about this is futile. Do her parents really think that the coach would suspend someone who scores as many points as she does? She's in great physical condition! This portrait shows a sixteen year old who has a strong desire to control her life herself. At the same time she has a limited ability to do so effectively. Her parents have tried keeping her at home following a curfew violation. Hannah went to bed on time, but then simply sneaked out of the house by climbing over the balcony. Increasing the punishment – grounding her for a whole month – led to terrible arguments, especially between Hannah and her father. Hannah's parents are facing a dilemma. They do not object to her going out as long as she respects the rules. They do not like being forced to impose stricter discipline because Hannah refuses to respect these rules.

Their list has only one item on it: coming home too late when she goes out. There is just one category. The inappropriate behaviour is persistent but her level of functioning is not low. Her parents not only hope to eliminate her inappropriate behaviour; they also want to challenge her by rewarding good behaviour. They need to find something their adolescent cares about. And what Hannah cares about is her pocket money.

Use the list below to choose the behaviour you want to work on.

3.1.a. Making a list

Do the following:
- Read the football metaphor on page 112, Appendix C
- Make a list of the child's inappropriate behaviour that you would like to work on; do this alone or together with other adults (partner, family member, teacher).
- Where possible, formulate it in terms of visible behaviour. Use the child's actual behaviour as your starting point. Do not use general terms such as "obey". Try to concentrate on specific examples such as "shouting at the table", "kicking", "pushing your brother", "doing homework", "coming home after twelve o'clock", "smoking pot on school nights", "stealing from our wallets".
- Check your list and replace interpretations and vague references with descriptions of actual behaviour.
- If more than one adult has worked on the list check whether it contains shared irritations or priorities.
- Use the following guidelines to draw up the list:
  - Behaviour during specific activities or in a specific place
  - Behaviour in certain groups
  - Behaviour aimed at specific people or specific things
  - Behaviour that occurs before, at or after a certain time
  - More worrying behaviour, less worrying behaviour
  - Behaviour that causes or potentially causes damage to people or things
  - Behaviour during escalations, tantrums or arguments
  - Behaviour related to agreed behaviour
  - Behaviour related to smoking, drinking or taking drugs.
- Add to the list if necessary

3.1.b. Choosing a category and subcategory

| Do the following:

- Accept that you cannot practice everything at once, just as you cannot practice all football moves at the same time during one training session.
- Take small steps.
- Look for behaviours that go together and place them in one group. We call this group a category.
- Choose a category to work on. Staying with the football metaphor, for example, you choose the corner, passing technique, head ball or penalty.
- Define several steps, or smaller issues, within the chosen category. We call these smaller steps and issues a subcategory. This is explained in the football metaphor on page 112, Appendix C. If you have chosen penalty shots as the category, choose a subcategory of the penalty: placement of the ball, contact with the ball, type of shot, choice of corner, etc.
- Practice only one subcategory at a time, but determine the order in which subcategories will be practiced. Accept that you can do nothing about the other subcategories for awhile.
- Do not start with the most difficult behaviour on the list. Give yourself time to practice interventions.

3.1.c. Determining the level of functioning

| Do the following:

Using the following guidelines to determine the level at which the child functions.

- *High level:* this is the level at which it is possible to discuss things with the child. The inappropriate behaviour is incidental. You can talk about correcting the behaviour and the child responds to the reprimand. You can explain why you think the behaviour is inappropriate and unwise. You can have content disputes with the child, and discuss alternative behaviour. You can make agreements with the child.

- *Mid level:* this is the level at which it is difficult to discuss things with the child. The inappropriate behaviour recurs repeatedly, even after you have discussed it. You can make agreements but the child has trouble keeping his word. Repeatedly having the same content-based arguments is fruitless. At this level of functioning you need to work on developing appropriate behaviour. The desired behaviour is broken down in to smaller, practicable parts. These small bits of appropriate behaviour are then practiced and given small rewards. We use this method in reward programmes for small children.

- *Low level:* this is the level at which inappropriate behaviour has disrupted relationships. No discussion is possible about the inappropriate behaviour. The child accepts no responsibility for the inappropriate behaviour. The child appears to be insensitive to reward and punishment. Reward programmes no longer work. The inappropriate behaviour is frequent and/or serious. At this level of functioning you need to work on scaling down the inappropriate behaviour.

Consider the following:

This chapter is about preparing an intervention. You start by choosing an inappropriate behaviour you want to work on. The first thing to do is make a list of a number of the child's inappropriate behaviours. This forces you to give a very precise description of the behaviour. However, sometimes it is difficult to formulate this or distinguish it from other inappropriate behaviour. Making this list helps you to recognise the various behaviours that are causing concern. It is alright if it initially lists a lot of overlapping issues. Arranging the behaviour categories then helps you to distinguish between the different types of inappropriate behaviour. You realise that you will not be able to tackle them all at once.

Behaviour has to be clearly formulated in order for you to work on it. The term "obey" is more difficult to understand than the term "not shouting". Because what exactly does "obey" mean? In turn, "not shouting" is less specific that the term "not hitting your mother". You and the child may not have same definition of "not shouting". You can train yourself to describe behaviour more precisely. If your list says the child is "disobedient", this description is too vague to practice with. What would you be practicing? Descriptions such as "doesn't listen", "lives in his own world", "does exactly as he pleases", "refuses to take anyone seriously", "is unpleasant to his grandmother", or "steals things" are all too vague. In addition, seemingly apt interpretations often do not reflect the exact, visible behaviour of the child. Examples include "acting up", "behaving childishly", "just like your uncle", "junky behaviour", or "totally ADHD".

It takes some practice to learn how to describe what you see. You will have to force yourself to become as precise as a police agent describing a crime scene. For example, "is disobedient" becomes: "If I ask William to get into the car for the school run, he goes into the lavatory and takes his time." "Steals things" becomes "Sharon steals money from her mother's wallet." "Lives in his own world" becomes "If Ryan hits his sister and we try to talk to him about it, he starts singing." "Does exactly as he pleases" becomes " Lewis never calls when he eats at his girlfriend's house."

Thinking in "if-then" terms can help adults to formulate the problem more precisely. "If this happens, then you can expect that behaviour". This forces you to describe behaviour in terms of actions you can actually observe, and therefore control and follow up on.

You then choose one issue from the list – a category – to work on. For example, you might choose "the situation during meals". It may be that you then encounter different types of inappropriate behaviour during meals, such as never showing up on time, burping, screaming, walking away during the meal, arguing with your brother, throwing food, interrupting others, These are the subcategories. You can choose the subcategory that irritates you most, or the one that seems the easiest to start with. Then you can devise an intervention that is specifically geared to that behaviour.

Let's say you choose the subcategory "fighting with your brother during meals". This too can be divided into smaller parts. For example, you want to start with scaling down the child's tendency to hit his brother. And then deal with his pushing, and after that his shouting at his brother. These subcategories are comparable to the elements of the penalty shot in the football metaphor (See page 112, Appendix C). In the football situation, it may be that a child has mastered placement of the ball, but cannot kick. The child may function at a different level for every aspect of the penalty. The different levels at which the child functions determine what you need to work on, and identify the realistic objectives of practicing penalty shots.

Keep in mind that you can only practice one subcategory at a time. You cannot practice all of the behaviour on the list at once. Just as you cannot practice head balls and penalty shots at the same time during a football training session. Accept that other inappropriate behaviours will continue for the time being. And if that behaviour crops up, you can respond in the "old" way. You can also tell the child this when you announce that you are going to practice.

You may find it very discouraging to be forced to limit yourself to just one subcategory of one category. There is so much inappropriate behaviour you want to work on! Moreover, different kinds of serious behavioural problems seems to require drastic measures that have an immediate effect. How can it help to work on such a small part of the problem? The answer lies in the metaphor "fences in the mud" (See page 113, Appendix C). At first it seems useless to place fences in the mud. All you see is mud, and no results. You will not understand how this works until you start to siphon the mud out of one of the fenced off areas. This metaphor implies that smaller portions are easier to practice on, and you will not overextend yourself doing so. Moreover, there is no method that can miraculously eliminate inappropriate behaviour all at once. So it is better to resign yourself to a training programme. And that implies that results can only be achieved gradually. When choosing which of the child's behaviour you want to work on, WHAT you choose is sometimes less important than the fact THAT you have chosen. The important thing is the techniques used to siphon off the mud, section by section.

Sometimes dividing behaviour into categories requires flexibility. The following situation may arise: the child no longer hits, pushes or shouts at his sister. But he has started stomping on her toes. "Because you didn't say I couldn't....!" You can simply add the "new" behaviour to the programme. If the child constantly seeks out behaviour that is not on the list, you can describe the behaviour a little less precisely. However if you use the vaguer description "everything we haven't practiced but which is in our opinion a form of bullying during meals" you will need to communicate very clearly.

You have now chosen a behaviour category from the list of inappropriate behaviours, and described subcategories within that category. The next step is to evaluate the level at which the child functions in relation to a particular subcategory.

Why is the term functioning level useful? Inappropriate behaviour on the part of the child appears to be intentional. If you accuse the child of intentionally misbehaving, you will be met with obstinacy. And the child's obstinacy then provokes its own form of punishment. In the previous chapter we saw how you can avoid contributing to escalations by interpreting unwillingness as incapacity. The child is incapable of showing more appropriate behaviour in certain circumstances. You assume that the child functions at a lower than age-appropriate level. We are not used to this. In our dealings with the child we usually assume that he is functioning at his age level: "You're twelve now, and I expect this from you". Or "You'll soon be in secondary school; that what's expected of you." However, children with seriously inappropriate behaviour do not function at that level. You need to take into account the possibility of a much lower level of functioning. If you do not, you are over-estimating the child's capacity. In other words, offering the child an age-based training is asking too much. Both you and the child can become frustrated. The vicious circle of powerlessness and anger quickly opens up again.

The system you learned to apply helps the child to get a better grip on his own behaviour, and to develop more capacity to behave differently. This is done in a coaching manner, and is always based on the actual level at which the child functions. Always keep the actual functioning level in mind, not the desired level. A tailor-made suit is based on actual measurements, and not on what one would like them to be. The adult makes an educated guess about the child's level of functioning: high, medium or low.

3.2. Design the intervention

Portrait of a younger child

Luke's parents have followed the instructions and designed a behaviour programme. They have held a work session at a pro-active moment. Luke has been told exactly what to expect if he pulls Jessica's hair. They will give him a brief warning, worded as follows: "Luke this a yellow card." If he does not stop within five seconds, a time-out will follow (See page 106, Appendix B, The Sanction). The parents spent a lot of time discussing it. The inappropriate behaviour does not only occur at mealtimes. It can happen throughout the day, and it is not always convenient to send Luke out into the hall. His parents have decided to allow Luke to watch only half of his favourite television programme that evening. He will have to spend the first half in his room, and one of the parents will call him when the time is up. If he pulls Jessica's hair again after this sanction, next time he will have to miss the entire programme. But they are still not comfortable with the situation. They see that although Luke no longer pulls Jessica's hair, he continues to hit, kick and tease her. When they take him aside to discuss this he says "That's not what you said". What are they to do? Do they really have to practice step-by-step while he continues to bully his sister. What should they do if Luke continually invents new ways of teasing his sister?

The parents in this portrait cannot afford to deal with just one category or subcategory of inappropriate behaviour. Even if they bundle several behaviours together they will not get much farther than, for example, Luke's behaviour during meals. They teach him not to kick her under the table, make nasty remarks or treat Jessica like a pig. But Luke will always find other ways of continuing to physically or verbally abuse his sister by saying "That's not what you said!"

What the parents can do is the following. They can agree that it is not ethical to carry out the programme in this manner. Luke has to stop abusing Jessica immediately. Too many of his behaviours are harmful to her. Luke is apparently unable to learn how to respect his sister's rights in this way. The parents interpret this as an indication that he functions at a lower level. This means that they will have to adapt their description of the inappropriate behaviour to this lower level of functioning. The parents will describe the inappropriate behaviour in more general terms. From now on "all behaviour that we think is harmful to Jessica" will immediately lead to a sanction. Luke's parents have to make it clear that it is up to them to decide whether behaviour is harmful. They will also protect Jessica by telling Luke that she will be obliged to report everything that takes place outside of their field of vision.

This portrait demonstrates that you first have to choose a category to work on. You then make an educated guess about the level at which the child functions. In addition, Luke's parents have to determine whether taking time to develop the programme will result in any direct damage. Can they afford to practice dealing with only small parts of his behaviour towards Jessica? If Luke functions at a low level, that is not possible. They will have to expand their definition of inappropriate behaviour to include "a general ban on touching Jessica." Later they can try to devise a more subtle approach.

Portrait of an older child

In relation to the issue of coming home on time, Hannah functions somewhere on the dividing line between a medium and a low level. When designing an intervention, you can devise a combination of developing appropriate behaviour and scaling down inappropriate behaviour. Where arguments with adolescents about bed times, going out, pocket money allowances and the rights the child claims are concerned, the intervention can be based on the child's age.

The parents take this age as positive starting point. Hannah is invited to take part in a work session. Her father tells her that they have thought about how to avoid treating her as a child they have to run after all the time. Hannah is now sixteen and the pocket money allowance for that age is higher than it currently is. But if she does not keep her end of the bargain, that bonus will be reduced. Hannah interrupts her father to say that she has agreed no such thing. Her father replies that he understands that she finds this annoying, but in their family, this is the curfew time that applies to a child of her age. Her father continues his story. Hannah's pocket money allowance will be increased by 20%. But the increase will be granted on an "if-then" basis. If Hannah does not respect the rules that apply to a sixteen year old, she will not be paid a sixteen-year-old's pocket money. In fact, her pocket money will be reduced by 20%. If she sticks to the rules in the coming period, she will have more money to spend. If she relapses after that, her parents can respond immediately.

In this situation, Hannah is taken seriously, but the sanction is also consistent. The parents accept her claim that she should be treated like a sixteen-year-old, but she will be rewarded on the basis of her level of functioning. Notice that they do not punish her by forbidding her to go out. You may not agree with the amount chosen – 20% – but the figure should not be too high. Hannah will not learn from the amount that is withheld, but from the consistent use of the relevant sanction. And parents can pay out or adjust the amount of allowance she " earns" each week without feeling like they are treating her as a child.

Now design your intervention, using the child's level of functioning as your starting point. You will learn about timing, and about the need to pay attention to the form of the intervention. For easy reference, some of the information needed to design interventions is included in the appendices so that the information will not get in your way when you are consulting the instructions in this part of the manual.

The three parts of the intervention will be designed in this chapter. The **pro-active moment** is the announcement of the sanction before the incident takes place. The **reactive moment** is the application of the sanction during the incident, and the **post-active moment** is the discussion of how the sanction went after the incident. The announcement, implementation and discussion of the sanction are described in chapters 4, 5 and 6.

3.2.a. Basing the intervention on the level of functioning

Do the following:
- Read the appendix on The Intervention (page 99, Appendix A)
- Read the appendix on The Sanction (page 105, Appendix B)
- Keep in mind that the actual level of functioning determines what you can practice and which goals are feasible.
- Keep in mind that the actual level of functioning determines how much the child can handle.
- Also keep in mind that each training subcategory has to be appropriate for the child's actual level of functioning. In terms of the football metaphor (See page 112, Appendix C), if you have decided to practice penalty shots it makes a difference whether you are working with a striker from the A team or a newcomer to the game. The two players require different training techniques.
- Choose a high-level intervention (discussion, explanation), a mid-level intervention (developing appropriate behaviour), or a low level intervention (scaling down inappropriate behaviour).
- You may have already had some degree of success with a programme aimed at using rewards such as stickers to develop better behaviour. If this is no longer successful, you can switch to a programme aimed at scaling back inappropriate behaviour, which is appropriate for a child with a lower level of functioning.

3.2.b. Timing the intervention

Do the following:
- Be *pro-active:*
  - Do not wait until an incident occurs to devise an intervention. If you are being forced to react, you are too late. This makes you feel powerless, angry and sad again.
  - Keep in mind that the actual sanction is less important than the fact that you have announced it in advance, imposed it, discussed it afterwards, and consistently continue to do so.
  - Remember that at the time of the incident the child is functioning at a much lower level. Make sure that everyone involved knows exactly what is going to happen at that moment.
  - Make good use of the time before the intervention. Choose a quiet moment to explain what will happen if the inappropriate behaviour occurs. This is your *work session* with the child. You need to **say what you mean**.
  - Think ahead to what you want to say during the work session. Keep it short and simple. Do this in three steps:
    1. speak to the child in growth-promoting language
    2. briefly explain your reasons
    3. announce the sanction

The practical implications of this are described in Chapter 4.

- Be *reactive*:
    - Keep in mind that your credibility with the child depends on doing what you have said you will do when inappropriate behaviour occurs. You need to **mean what you say**.
    - Decide not to use the reactive moment to explain what you are going to do. Decide not to argue with the child at that moment. What is going to happen should be made clear in advance.
    - Do not choose punishment that is too severe and designed to "teach the child a good lesson". Choose a smaller sanction that can be applied consistently and if necessary repeated.
    - Choose one of the sanctions listed on page 106, Appendix B for the reactive moment. These include variations of the time-out concept.

  The practical implications of this are described In chapter 5.

- Be *post-active*:
    - Use the time following the incident. Prepare to hold a brief discussion after the incident of the inappropriate behaviour and the response to the sanction.
    - Do not stress the results, whether things went well in the end or whether the intervention failed. Instead, emphasise the child's efforts to take control of his own behaviour. Remember that this is a training situation. You discuss how the training went, not the results of the game.
    - Keep in mind that the post-active intervention is intended to encourage the child to think about his own behaviour and its consequences for himself. The child functioning at a lower level may find it difficult or impossible to think about the consequences of his behaviour for someone else.
    - Be prepared to speak to the child in growth-promoting language during the post-active phase, referring to progress made or things that still need work.

  The practical implications of this are described in Chapter 6.

3.2.c. Shaping the intervention

Do the following:
- Read the appendix on growth-promoting language (page 113, Appendix C).
- Keep in mind that the way in which you announce, implement and discuss an intervention is part of the training. A child with a serious behavioural problem will withdraw if he is constantly faced with an angry adult.
- Keep in mind that you have to practice speaking to the child in growth-promoting language. Practice in front of a mirror, when you are walking or driving. Ask yourself whether you are using the training language or if there is hidden anger in your choice of words.
- Use growth-promoting language during both the pro-active phase and the post-active work session.
- Speak to the child in a neutral, friendly tone of voice during the reactive moment.
- Take into account that the child may have suggestions of his own regarding the form of the sanctions. Think of this as a test of your own work attitude. Consider whether this should lead to an adjustment of your intervention in the design phase.
- Think about the combination of pro active, reactive and post active while you are devising an intervention. Mentally practice giving the training.

Consider the following:

We are now at the stage in the programme in which we design an intervention. Both the design and implementation of the intervention require the use of communicative instruments. You will learn how to use these instruments just as you have learned how to use a knife, fork and spoon. The relevant communicative instruments are: content, process and form. The programme also teaches you how to work with derived terms: level of functioning, timing and growth-promoting language. Read about this on page 99, Appendix A, The Intervention.

The real question here is how to design interventions for children when you have already tried so many strategies, and nothing ever seems to work. We now know that children with serious behavioural problems do not function at an age-appropriate level. What are the practical implications of this for designing an intervention? How do you deal with a lower level of functioning? What things do you need to take into account? What can you expect? The success of the intervention is directly related to how accurately you assess the child's level of functioning. This is something you need to keep in mind when designing your interventions. A football trainer adapts his training schedule to the capacities of his players. So practice assessing the actual level at which the child functions. Ensuring the programme is attuned to the child's actual capacity can prevent a lot of frustration and loss of time.

Of course if the problem is serious enough, we all have a tendency to resort to more severe punishments, content disputes and angry attitudes. You need to understand while it is perfectly natural to respond in this way, it is not effective. Children who function at a low level are not inclined to learn from the severity, length, or scope of a sanction. These kinds of sanctions usually only make it more difficult to reach the child. And they reinforce the power struggle. The child often wins the power struggle because he is able to manipulate you into a passive work position. And as an adult in a passive work position you will be inclined to impose even stricter punishments. The child will then announce that he "doesn't care" about the punishment. And that makes you discouraged and inclined to do nothing at all, since nothing helps. A child functioning at a low level learns nothing from harsh punishment designed to "teach the child a lesson once and for all." The child learns from the consistent application of smaller sanctions that have been announced in advance, and from discussing them afterwards. That is why you need to develop a training programme that is based on the actual level at which the child functions, and not on the level at which it is supposed to function. Or the level at which he is able to function once in a great while. You accept the current level of functioning with a certain equanimity, and then you gear your training to that level.

The question is how do you get started and how do you prevent the problems from recurring? Timing, and using growth-promoting language make it possible for you to do things differently. This is explained in more detail below.

We will start with the question of timing. There are three main time frames: before, during and after the incident. You can use these three times to devise interventions. The pro-active moment makes it clear in advance what the child can expect if he shows inappropriate behaviour. The reactive moment is the point at which the inappropriate behaviour occurs, and you do exactly what you have said you would do. The post-active moment helps you to discuss the incident as if it were part of a training session the child is participating in.

You have repaired your work attitude and can therefore start work at these three moments. There is now less pressure on the previously tense reactive moment because you are expecting it. You have designed a training plan, and will be discussing the relevant action afterwards. The reactive moment now has the support of the partial interventions that take place before and after it. If you only make use of sanctions in the reactive moment, you are ill-prepared for the child's serious behavioural problems. You are the one opening the door to an angry, powerless and therefore passive work attitude. Moreover, the child is functioning at a low level, particularly at that reactive moment. You cannot expect him to adopt a listening, learning attitude.

Timing ensures that you do not leave things until the moment of the incident. It goes without saying that you are too late if you have not started thinking about an intervention until the behaviour occurs. That is why you and the child prepare for the inappropriate behaviour. And you become accustomed to discussing the intervention with the child afterwards. Discussing the situation before and after intervention in growth-promoting language emphasises the training aspect of the intervention, and helps both you and the child to avoid thinking in terms of punishment and retribution. Timing is therefore a valuable training instrument, also for yourself. It trains the trainer. And training the trainer is precisely what helps you to break out of the vicious circle created by a passive work attitude.

Do not feel bad about training just one behaviour, or about only being able to impose one sanction at a time. You are also in training, and that takes time.

In addition to timing the intervention, it is also very important to think about the form it takes. Read about growth-promoting language on page 113, Appendix C. It is essential to realise that this language motivates both you and the child. During neutral, pro-active moments growth-promoting language is an instrument that shows respect for the child. It makes a distinction between the child and the inappropriate behaviour. During the post-active moment, the same language places a positive label on the child's efforts to control his behaviour. Again, this emphasises the training aspect of the intervention. The combination of timing and growth-promoting language takes some of the pressure off the reactive moment. Everyone is prepared for the inappropriate behaviour and the sanction. The reactive moment can now be seen as a training moment as well. This creates a better work climate than anxiously waiting for an incident to occur and not knowing what to do when it does.

Interventions involving younger children will take a different form than those involving older children. In the design phase, we can take frequent forms of inappropriate behaviour into account. Read about this in the appendices on The Intervention (page 101, Appendix A) and The Sanction (page 105, Appendix B).

These are some of the questions you need to ask:
How do you respond to the child's different reactions to an intervention? Do you take the older child's need for autonomy into account? What do you do if the intervention does not result in an improvement? What do you do about the behaviour of other children? As the adult, what do you do if it is just not your day? What do you do about comments by family members? As the school, what do you do if the parents do not recognise the problem? As parents, what do you do if the school has no policy on this?

Always remember that the child will not be happy with the intervention you have devised. The lower the level of functioning, the lower the amount of cooperation. During pro-active moments the child will try to argue about the usefulness of interventions, or the justification for them. He may try to boycott your programme of interventions and sanctions, saying "Who cares about your plans?" Or he may try to negotiate the terms of the intervention. The child can also devise a plan he thinks is better than your plan. These suggestions should be regarded as the child's attempt to hold on to his position of power. They should also be regarded as a test of your own work attitude, so keep this in mind when you are devising and carrying out interventions. It is of course easier to respond harshly and end up with the usual escalations. It is also easier to carry on long discussions about reasonableness, and so to avoid intervening. It helps if the trainer recognises that the training is difficult for the child.

Another pitfall can occur during the post-active moment. You need to suppress the urge to talk about the "game results". Examples of this are saying things such as "You see, you can do it," or "If only you could do this during meals...!", or "Next time if you would just think before you start to shout." Imagine what would happen if after a successful training session, the football coach said "If only you would play so well in the game...!" This may have a motivating effect on a child functioning at high level, but it will paralyse a child with a behavioural problem who functions at a low level. The trainer is referring to a level that the child cannot achieve, and this places huge pressure on the child. The post-active comments become a humiliating "you bin" experience (See page 116, Appendix C). The child picks up on your anger. The danger is that the child will then start to function at an even lower level, which in turn will elicit more angry powerlessness on the part of the trainer.

Once a particular aspect of behaviour has sufficiently improved, you can move on to the next subject. Do not count on a higher level of functioning because training the previous subject went well. Do not hesitate to resume training an aspect of behaviour that has already shown improvement if the level of functioning decreases. This can be result of your being too lax in your application of the programme (See Chapter 6.4.b.). But a lower level of functioning may also be the result of a childhood psychiatric condition. A child's level of functioning can change rapidly.

Designing an intervention comes down to the following:
You take stock of inappropriate behaviour and repair your own work attitude if necessary. You then make a list with exact descriptions of the inappropriate behaviour. You choose one project from the list. You assess the level of functioning. If it is too low, choose a strategy aimed at scaling down the behaviour. You hold a pro-active work session with the child, during which you speak in growth-promoting language. You tell the child what will happen if the inappropriate behaviour occurs. When it does occur, you give a warning. If the behaviour recurs or does not stop during the agreed period, the sanction follows. The sanction is often a form of time-out. After the sanction you welcome the child with growth-promoting language. However, if the inappropriate behaviour recurs, you behave consistently, giving a warning and imposing a sanction if necessary.

In this chapter, we collected our thoughts about shaping an intervention. It became clear that there is a fixed system for determining the intervention. However, because behavioural problems vary from one situation to the next, it is never possible to devise a standard intervention. It is not the substance of the intervention, but the way in which it is arrived at that can be standardised.

The next three chapters deal with the implementation of the programme. We start with the practical aspects of the pro-active intervention in Chapter 4.

4. Hold a work session using growth-promoting language

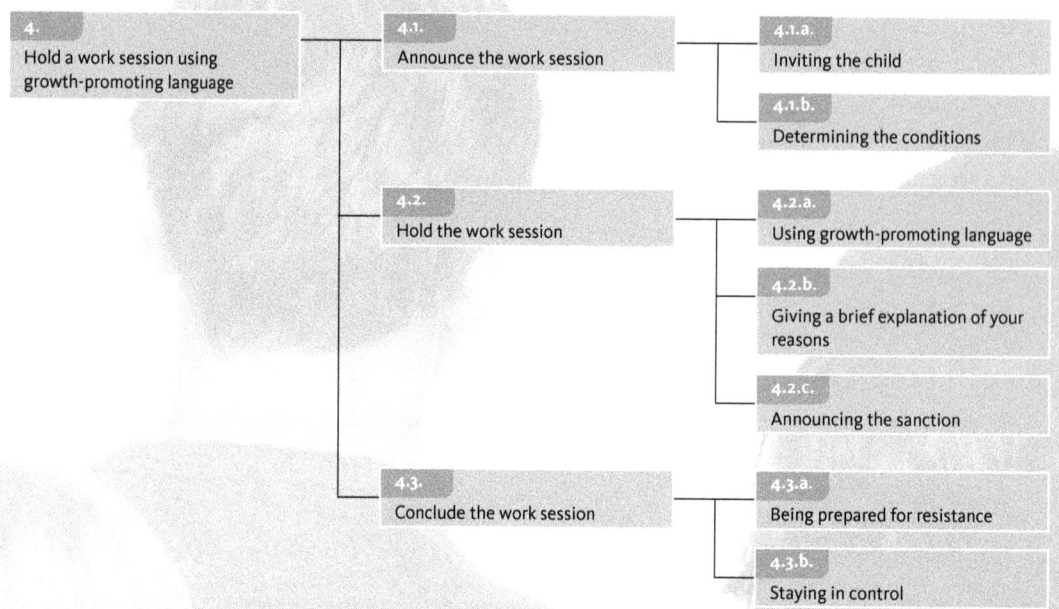

What is this chapter about?

When inappropriate behaviour occurs it must be clear to both you and the child what the intervention is going to be. You tell the child in advance what the intervention is during a work session. Even if the child functions at a low level, he will pay more attention if you speak to him in growth-promoting language. This chapter helps you to prepare a work session.

4. Hold a work session using growth-promoting language

Portrait of a younger child
"You see, that's what I mean"
Timothy is 11 and in his last year of primary school. He bicycles to school every day. He is not an easy child, but right now things are going reasonably well at home and at school. The problem is that he refuses to put his bicycle in the garage. Timothy has had plenty of warnings from his father about theft and the fact that money does not grow on trees. One week he had to walk to school because his parents had locked up his bicycle. This was meant to teach Timothy a lesson, and for a week things went well.

Portrait of an older child
"I don't want to hear about it!"
The parents of fifteen-year-old Bethany have invited her to a work session. Even before the talk begins, Bethany realises that the meeting is going to be about a kind of programme to change her behaviour. She says, "I don't want to hear about it." Her father is not prepared for this. He had planned to explain the programme in a friendly tone. But he doesn't even get the chance. Bethany draws her father into a heated discussion, a battle that is being fought with her weapons. Her father then talks to her for twenty minutes about the substance of the problems. The result is that Bethany achieves a hollow victory over her father; he is beaten but she takes nothing away from the discussion. The parents want to restore the hierarchy. But Bethany succeeds in destabilising her father from the start by announcing that she is not going to listen.

Introduction
The following chapters deal with the implementation of the intervention. A good intervention uses three points in time: **before** the incident (chapter 4), **during** the incident (chapter 5) and **after** the incident (chapter 6). We use these three points in time and call them the pro-active, reactive and post-active parts of the intervention.

This chapter deals with the pro-active part of the intervention.

You can continue to hope that the inappropriate behaviour will not recur. You can also continue to trust that the child's behaviour will improve following a previous discussion. If you are then caught off guard by the inappropriate behaviour, that is the reactive moment. At that moment you do not have the tools that pro-active intervention provides. In addition, you are forced to do another reactive intervention. You are responding to behaviour that you hoped would not happen again. And you are always one step behind with your response. Letting yourself be pinned to the reactive moment means living between hope and fear. A good day gives you hope that things will be better now. A bad day causes you to fear that things will never get better. You become trapped in the vicious circle that perpetuates the disappointment, anger and powerlessness. Within that vicious circle, your only choices are between "black" and "white" interventions.

The pro-active intervention gives you the opportunity to show the child that you have repaired your own work attitude. You know that the behaviour will recur and you are prepared for it. You take the initiative to talk about the inappropriate behaviour at a moment when it is not occurring. You are not under pressure at that moment. Perhaps you have even decided not to let yourself be pressured any longer.

The project you have prepared is presented in a brief, friendly manner. You pay close attention to how you approach the child. You do not speak to the child in punitive, sarcastic, ironic or angry tones, but in growth-promoting language. The concept of growth-promoting language is explained on page 113, Appendix C. In spite of the friendly tone, the child is being informed of a strict behavioural programme. You understand the child does not have to like this. The child is not the one who wants an intervention that links consequences to inappropriate behaviour. You take the possibility of the child's resistance to any kind of change into account.

You learn that it is important to use the pro-active and post-active moment. Doing so systematically will give you some breathing space at the moment when the inappropriate behaviour occurs. Now both you and the child know exactly what will happen during the reactive moment, because it has been announced in a pro-active way. It is a question of **saying what you mean and meaning what you say**. If you learn how to use the interventions during the pro-active and the post-active moments, you can teach yourself to deal with inappropriate behaviour in a more professional manner.

What does it mean learning how to deal with inappropriate behaviour more professionally? It means learning not to be surprised time and again by inappropriate behaviour. You are prepared for it. You learn to not only think about it when it happens. This keeps you from being drawn into the vicious circle when the behaviour occurs at a reactive moment. It enables you to put some distance between yourself and the inappropriate behaviour so that you can practice another approach. You train yourself to train the child. Using the three points in time helps you to take an active position. That is a better starting point than clinging to the hope that the inappropriate behaviour will not happen again and then finding yourself pinned down in the reactive moment.

4.1. Announce the work session

Portrait of a younger child

Timothy's parents have learned the method described in the book. They are ready to get started and anxious to see whether it will work. One Sunday afternoon Timothy is asked to take part in a work session. He is intrigued. His parents are usually angry with him and he is not interested in their arguments. Now they seem friendly. Moreover, there is nothing for them to get angry about at this moment.

Portrait of an older child

What could Bethany's father have done? Let's look at a scenario in which Bethany tries to remain in control and in which her father is prepared for this. This time she accomplished this by disrupting the announcement of the work session, but she could have done so during or after the work session. When Bethany says she doesn't want to listen, and her father is prepared for this, he can respond immediately. He can say that he wants to stop treating her like a small child, and that is why he wants to choose a quiet moment to talk to her. If Bethany still does not want to listen, her father closes the matter. He regards this behaviour as a sign that she is functioning at a lower level. He says, "Okay, I see you're not interested now, we'll try later, or tomorrow." When she then tries to coax him into a discussion, or pressures her father to tell her what he wanted to say, he refuses. He says, "That is exactly what I want to avoid. I'll find another moment to talk to you." This puts him in charge of the situation.

> *Bethany may now suspect that her father wants to take back control. She may make another attempt to bait her father and make him angry. Her father can then say: "You can carry on badgering me, but we'll talk about it later." He refuses to argue with her. If several attempts to hold a work session are unsuccessful, the father will stop trying. He says, "Okay, I see that it is difficult to have a discussion. On Monday we'll start doing things differently."*
>
> *In this example, Bethany's father makes good use of the three points in time. It starts with a moment when he invites her to take part in a **pro-active** work session. If she continues to refuse he does a **reactive** intervention, but one that is aimed at Bethany's uncooperative behaviour. He subsequently adds the **post-active** remark: "It is still difficult to have a discussion." Finally, he turns the **post-active** moment into a pro-active moment by announcing that starting on Monday things will be different.*

Now announce the pro-active work session. Make sure you speak to the child in a friendly but firm tone.

4.1.a. Inviting the child

Do the following:
- Invite the child to participate in a friendly, decisive manner.
- Never choose a reactive moment to invite the child.
- Use the neutral terms work session or discussion.
- Prepare for a lack of cooperation from the child. The child may even refuse to accept the invitation. You can then say that you want to discuss the matter in an adult fashion, without punishment and arguments. You let this sink in for a short while and announce that you will come back to it later.
- If the child continues to refuse to talk about matters, you can immediately switch to a shortened version of the work session. For example: "I have thought about your behaviour and the arguments it causes and about how we are going to deal with it as from Monday."
- If the child still refuses, you can say that you respect that. You indicate that you are taking the child seriously by discussing what the reaction to the behaviour will be. This gives the child a renewed opportunity to take part in the work session.
- If the child still refuses you can say: "Let me know if you want to hear what I have to say. But things are still going to be different on Monday."

4.1.b. Determining the conditions

Do the following:
- Announce a work session and plan for it to happen at a quiet moment. For example, on Sunday afternoon over a cup of tea. At school, choose a time after class when you can talk to the child in private.
- If the child decides that he wants to hold the work session **now** or at another time of his choosing, continu to set the conditions yourself. You can hold the child to your own time schedule.
- The child may refuse to let you set the conditions of the work session. The child may be very insistent, demanding to know right now what this is about. Stop the negotiations immediately and say you will come back to this later; the whole purpose of the work session is to avoid discussing matters in an argumentative way. Cheerfully stand your ground, even if the child continues to pressure you.

Consider the following:

The intervention starts when you announce the work session. That is why it is important to think carefully about it. The term work session is neutral, and it emphasises that you want to discuss things. That is less intimidating than punitive talk or stressing how serious the matter is. Instead of asking or inviting the child to participate you announce that you are going to have a work session. This is the *first* sign that you are taking back control and restoring the hierarchy. Fixing a specific time for the work session is the *second sign* that you are taking back control and restoring the hierarchy. You set the conditions.

Younger children are usually intrigued by the announcement of a work session. It gives them an exceptional position with a label that applies to adults: work session. An older child will either have no objection or be wary. If the child is wary or refuses to participate, calmly make it clear that the work session will take place and is not dependent on the child's will. In this way you emphasise your own position as the trainer. Remember that announcing the intervention and the work session will have little effect if you use them when the child is at his worst (the reactive moment). Or if you are extremely angry. Ensure that you can set the conditions by taking this into account.

It is important to understand that even an invitation to a work session will make some children recalcitrant. The child will be reluctant to give up his position of power. Any expression on your part that deviates from the familiar pattern can make the child curious, but also wary. You understand this. The child is seeing a remarkable change in your work attitude. Instead of being an opponent who is easily manoeuvred into a powerless position you now announce a work session in a calm, friendly but firm tone. Furthermore, the work session is not taking place now, but at a later moment. You are apparently taking time for this. Why the sudden change? Introducing time as a factor is an intervention in itself. Taking your time with this helps you to become less tense, and the child's position of power starts to crumble.

It is important to announce a work session, even in serious situations. You may wonder if this is possible. A very serious, physically threatening situation has to be stopped externally, sometimes even with the help of the police. There may be many situations that come close to this in terms of their seriousness in which the adults do not ask for outside help. Or in which police find a child that has just calmed down. In addition, the confrontation with the child's seriously inappropriate behaviour can throw you off balance again. Once again, you are pinned down in the reactive moment. These are situations that are difficult to see as "training". And this programme will probably not be the first thing that comes to mind. But even in such situations, you can take a little time to regroup and start with the programme by introducing time as a factor and turning the reactive moment into a pro-active moment. You do this by announcing a work session. Introducing time as a factor allows you to turn an overwhelming reactive moment into a pro-active moment. As the adult you can take back control and set the conditions yourself, even in "impossible" situations.

4.2. Hold the work session

Portrait of a younger child

At the beginning of the discussion, Timothy's parents tell him that they no longer wish to treat him as a small child. Timothy is glad that his parents have decided not to be so lame. It doesn't work anyway! His mother says they have thought of something that will keep them from having so many arguments. That should improve the home environment. All the arguing is bad for his younger sister Alice and his little brother Ben. He is old enough now to start thinking a little about these things. Timothy interrupts his mother to say that Alice is often the one who starts arguing. She does things that make him very angry. Last week she went into his room and broke off a whole piece of his Lego castle. She doesn't look where she's going. And she's not supposed to be in Timothy's room anyway. He has told her so many times. Stupid girl! The mother allows herself to be drawn into the discussion, saying, "That is exactly what I mean!" She launches into a lecture on how it is time for Timothy to learn not to be so negative about other people. Starting with his little sister. Timothy needs to understand that he will not be able to get away with this in secondary school. In no time the focus of the conversation has switched to his arguments with Alice and Ben. Wasn't it supposed to be about putting his bicycle in the garage?

This portrait illustrates how careful you have to be about explaining too much in the pro-active phase. Your explanations may be well-intentioned, but explanations are "substance" and this only works with children who function at a higher level. The mother is contributing to the problem. She has linked the announcement of a project about putting his bicycle in garage to arguments with his brother and sister and the home environment. In more difficult situations, a very brief explanation is sufficient. The child should not be given any openings for further discussion. The brief explanation can be very simple. With regard to putting his bicycle in the garage Timothy's mother could have said: "And I know you need your bicycle." This is a fairly value-free statement, which is not open to discussion.

Portrait of an older child

Bethany's curiosity gets the better of her. During mealtime she casually asks her father: "Didn't you want to talk to me? When is that?" Her father immediately seizes the opportunity to set the conditions, but also to respect her autonomy. He says, "How about this evening between nine and half past nine?" Bethany agrees. The work session is about Bethany's bad behaviour at school. She shouts at teachers and storms out of the classroom if she feels offended. According to the coordinator, it is impossible to talk to her when this happens. Bethany's father knows he has to keep it short at this point, and above all avoid lecturing her. He speaks to her in growth-promoting language: " I have thought about what I heard from your coordinator, but you're right, we need to do something different. No more nagging and lecturing. You're too old for that." Then he gives her a somewhat vague, short explanation: "Everyone has to learn how to deal with conflicts at some point." He then announces what Bethany can expect. "I am not going to follow you around nagging. I will be meeting with your coordinator once a week. You will have the chance to go to the teacher you walked out on and try to solve the problem. And every Sunday afternoon we will have a brief work session about how things are going."

> *The father is using the process box. Read about this on page 109, Appendix B. He gives her time, but he also makes it clear that the leeway she has is limited to one week. Every week he will ask both Bethany and the coordinator how her behaviour has been. Now things can go either way. Bethany may try to approach a teacher after an incident. She will be praised for this. Or after a month her interpretation may still be different from that of her coordinator. Her father will then confront her with the fact that although he is treating her as an adult, she is behaving like a child. In this portrait there is no clear sanction. But Bethany knows exactly what to expect. And her father has used a well-prepared pro-active intervention to take control of the situation.*

Now hold the work session. Speak to the child in growth-promoting language, briefly explain your reasons, and announce the sanction.

4.2.a. Using growth-promoting language

Do the following:

- Read about growth-promoting language on page 113, Appendix C.
- Start the work session by speaking to the child in growth-promoting language. Use sentences such as: "I actually think you are too old to have me chasing around after you like a police officer." Or: "We successfully completed the previous programme, now you're ready for the next step." Or: "I've been thinking about it, and you're right.... we will try something else."
- Check whether your tone is ironic or sarcastic. For example: "Because you behave like a child...," "or: "Because I am really tired of having to treat you like a child ..."
- Keep in mind that the child is not enthusiastic about listening to you.
- Expect the child to say things that will throw you off guard.
- Think of everything the child now says as an attempt to take back control. Do not let yourself be goaded into content disputes or nasty remarks. If you notice yourself veering off course, start again and say to the child: "Look, I'm doing it too now. We need to do things differently. I am taking a five minute break and then we'll start again".
- If the child tries to continue arguing about substantive matters, or tries to "you-bin" (See page 116, Appendix C) say: "I understand that you don't like it, but we are still going to do it."

4.2.b. Giving a brief explanation of your reasons

Do the following:

- After speaking in growth-promoting language, briefly explain your reasons for doing an intervention.
- Keep it simple.
- The explanation can be a bit vague.
- Use positive sentences such as: "And I know we all want to enjoy sitting down to a meal," or "And because you are older now, it is time to do things differently".
- A good rule of thumb is to start the sentence with: "And I know that..."
- Practice this in advance to avoid getting caught up in long explanations.

4.2.c. Announcing the sanction

Do the following
- Use the **say what you mean and mean what you say** principle.
- Keep to the following sequence:
  - Start by referring to the brief explanation using a sentence such as: "And I am going to help you with this, and this is how we are going to do it…"
  - Clearly specify what the inappropriate behaviour is. Always describe this in terms of the behaviour you see. Do not be vague and do no interpret behaviour. Say, for example: "When I see that you kick your sister under the table", and not: "When I see that you are not mature enough to sit at the table… "Say, for example: "I want you to come to the table within five minutes of being called…" and not "If you disobey…" If necessary, practice this with other adults.
  - Say that you will give a sign as soon as you see this behaviour. You can call this a yellow card. If the behaviour does not stop within the time period you specify, a sanction will follow.
  - Be clear about what you will do if the child displays this behaviour. Make sure you have thought of the sanctions beforehand, otherwise you run the risk of imposing a less appropriate sanction or one that cannot be enforced. Keep the sanction simple, and limited in terms of length and harshness.
  - Also be clear about when the programme will start. Be specific about the time of the next work session.
  - If asked, say that training will continue until the relevant behaviour has improved.

Consider the following

A work session can be very short. Sometimes only a minute or two are needed. The boy who hits his sister at the table can be addressed as follows: "I really think you are too old to have me following you around nagging (growth-promoting language) and I know that we all want to enjoy our meal together (brief explanation), so I am going to help you, and this is how we are going to do it (restore the hierarchy). Every time you hit your sister, or pretend to, you will get a yellow card. If you do it again on the same day, I will take a half an hour off your television watching time (announce the intervention)."

As the adult you may object to such a lenient sanction for hitting his sister. You want it to stop right away. It is simply not acceptable! This is an understandable reaction. But the child has learned nothing from earlier, harsher punishments. And this intervention is part of a more extensive programme.

Why is speaking growth-promoting language important? A child who often demonstrates inappropriate behaviour is used to being scolded. He has become accustomed to closing himself off from this. This mechanism comes into operation as soon as the child suspects that he is going to get another lecture, that he is going to be asked again why he has misbehaved, that punishment will follow, or that he is considered to be a bad child. The child has learned to protect himself against this, and pretends to be indifferent. It is therefore essential to pay attention to the way in which you speak to the child. The old way was ineffective. The child will not be open to more anger or to cynicism and sarcasm, no matter how carefully packaged it is. That is why it is useful to practice speaking growth-promoting language.

Growth-promoting language is more considerate. It is friendly and you show respect for the child with the behavioural problem. Growth-promoting language is a constant reminder to you to use a developmental model instead of a punitive model. However, growth-promoting language is not indulgent language. You are not pandering to the child or candy-coating the message. Growth-promoting language does not make excuses. There is a strategic side to growth-promoting language, because when you tell a teenager that you no longer want to treat him as a child, you are actually saying much more. You are indirectly telling him that in the recent past you have apparently felt you had to treat him like a child. There was a reason for this. You are labelling his behaviour childish, even though he is a teenager. You are also announcing that you now intend to treat him in an age-appropriate fashion, even if he behaves childishly. He can continue to do so but now it will have consequences. This one sentence also tells him that you would like your relationship with him to be more age-appropriate. You acknowledge his autonomy, but you also challenge him to respect the boundaries. Finally, this is also a subtle way of letting him know that you are in a position to take in the entire situation, and that you will be keeping a close eye on things.

The instructions tell you to give a brief reason for your intervention. During the work session, it is important to avoid over-long descriptions of why you are doing an intervention. There is no need to spend a lot of time thinking up the perfect justification. It is better to keep it short and somewhat general. In an attempt to hold on to his power, the child will weigh up every word. The child will quickly find the weak spot in your line of reasoning, especially if you are doing your best to explain everything. Keep in mind that the child functions at a level at which discussion and an understanding of the other person's arguments are not elf-evident. For the boy who is picking on his sister at the table, it is enough to say, "And I know that we all want to enjoy sitting down to a meal".

Sometimes, however, you may feel forced to comment. If so, remember that the real reason for the intervention is that as parents you have the obligation to give the child a proper upbringing. Telling the child this confronts him with the fact that adults are not allowed to neglect a child. Putting it this way suggests that not doing the intervention would be to neglect the child. You separate the reason for the intervention from the child and his behaviour. Adults simply have an obligation to educate the child. That is the law, and it is beyond your control. You accept your responsibility as an adult to educate the child. The child can argue all he wants about the intervention and the reasons for it, it is still going to happen. At school or in other groups, the adults have the same obligation.

When you announce the sanction, it is important to give a clear description of the inappropriate behaviour and of the expected consequences. However, it is not always easy to describe to the child exactly what the inappropriate behaviour is. This is something you need to think about during the design phase (See chapter 3). Sometimes you notice that two problems are inter-related, for example picking on a sister during meals and complaining about the food. If this only becomes clear during a practice session, it can simply be split up into two projects. After that it depends on the child's level of functioning whether or not they can be practiced at the same time or separately.

The general rule is that you describe what the child **does** or **does not** do. The focus should be on behaviour. Instead of saying "behaving at the table", say "making unpleasant remarks about the food before the meal is over". Do not talk about "respecting other people's things" but about "taking money from a wallet". Not "learning to accept responsibility" but "being home before 1 am". The child needs to know exactly what his boundaries are.

4.3. Conclude the work session

Portrait of a younger child

Timothy's parents have devised a plan to encourage him to put his bicycle in the garage. However, during the work session his mother gets drawn into arguments about why he fights with Alice and Ben. His father helps her out. He says, "That's a good example of how things usually go. We are having this work session so that we can start doing things differently. This is how we are going to do it." This is a graceful way of taking back control of the work session. It is as if Timothy is again being spoken to in growth-promoting language. He can then go on to give a short justification for the programme. "We know how much you need your bicycle." He announces the sanction which the parents have agreed on in advance. If Timothy's bicycle is still in the garden one hour after he comes home, he will be given a warning. If after ten minutes the bicycle is still outside, he will be sent to bed half an hour earlier that same evening. Regardless of what is on the television, and regardless of whether he has football training. Timothy makes another attempt to convince his father of the injustice of this. He argues that they are the ones who want him to take part in sports every week because it is so good for him. And it will be their fault if he can't participate. His father says: "I understand that it will be difficult at first, but this is how it is going to be. The programme starts this coming Monday." When his father asks him if everything is clear to him, Timothy makes one last effort, this time becoming angry and saying that they always pick on him. His father does not give an ironic response, or make a joke. He cheerfully closes the work session and goes off to do something else. His mother asks if anyone would like a cup of tea.

Portrait of an older child

Bethany has just had a pro-active work session. Her father has told her what she can expect, and what is expected of her. Her mother was also present during the work session. The programme starts tomorrow. She is a bit surprised at the united front her parents present. From force of habit she starts to argue about the measure, which she does not really think is necessary. The behaviour her parents are referring to was provoked by someone else at school, but it is no longer an issue. To her surprise, her parents do not respond to her efforts to argue with them. Bethany tries a different tactic. "This is so childish! Don't expect me to go along with it." Her father replies in a friendly tone, "Yes, I think it's very childish too. And I hope that it will not be necessary for long." The conversation ends here.

Now conclude the pro-active work session. Be prepared for the child's protestations. Also take into account your own emotions and convictions. They can recreate the old situation. Make sure you take control and keep it.

4.3.a. Being prepared for resistance

Do the following:
- Assume that the child will object to the announced intervention.
- Do not respond in a weary, angry or disappointed manner.
- Be prepared for objections in the form of stubborn refusal to take part, walking away, feigned indifference, insults.
- But also be prepared for arguments and promises that without the programme things will really be different this time.

- Expect the child to want to discuss the matter, or even respond with enthusiasm. The child may offer his own ideas.
- Know that you can expect a reaction and do not waste your energy being upset about it.

4.3.b. Staying in control

Do the following:
- Conclude the work session with a brief, friendly remark.
- Let the child know you hear and acknowledge his objections, but that you are not going to respond to them.
- For example say, "Yes, it will take some getting used to" or "I understand that this is different for you, but this is how we are going to do it."
- Clearly state that you will be doing what you said you would do, but that after a while you will consider whether any adjustments need to be made.
- If the child continues to ask questions, wants to argue or tries to make you angry, see this as an attempt to remain in control.
- Do not be tempted to make additional explanations.
- Calmly end the work session. Say, for example, "We are going to stop now, but we will come back to this later."

Consider the following:

The work session will now end. A plan has been introduced. The child sees that your behaviour in relation to the inappropriate behaviour has changed: you have spoken to the child in growth-promoting language, but you have stood your ground. That is new for the child. It is understandable that he is not sure where he stands now. The child will test whether your work attitude really has changed. And whether you not only say what you mean, but also mean what you say. Be prepared for the child's objections once the intervention has been announced.

Objections can take many forms. The child may want to discuss matters. Or even suggest a better plan. He may solemnly promise that the inappropriate behaviour will not happen again. The child's response can be angry or indifferent. You do not have to be disappointed about this. You should not make any attempt to convince the child that it is all for his own good. Assume that the child has a stake in maintaining the status quo. And do not forget that the child is functioning at a level that makes content disputes futile. That is why it is useless to explain the plan yet again. If you let the child goad you into giving a better explanation of your approach, you are placing yourself in his favourite territory. A child with serious behavioural problems has had a lot of practice with confrontation. This applies to both younger and older children.

Keep in mind that you may feel the urge to raise your own objections. You may find it difficult to intervene. You do not want to be as strict as your parents were. Or you do not want to become like your partner or ex-partner. You might be very busy at work right now. Or think it is someone else's turn to take responsibility. There are many possible reasons for making objections. However, it is important to understand that this can cause the programme to stagnate by creating a comfortable situation in which you remain in a passive position and continue to complain. It also provides an excuse for not practicing the programme.

"It doesn't work anyway…" It is a more comfortable situation for the child as well if he is able to influence you with arguments, promises, inaccessibility or anger. Then the child will easily be able to maintain his position of power in the educational situation. So be prepared for objections in the first phase of implementing the programme: your own as well as the child's.

It is important to maintain control when ending the work session. In practice this means being aware of things that can take away your control. A familiar pitfall is having a "nice talk" with the child. At this stage, "nice talks" with the child can undermine the programme. As adults we have a tendency to feel hopeful if we are able to have a good discussion with a child who has behavioural problems. We are happy that after so much unpleasantness, the child is prepared to sit quietly and listen. And we tend to think the child now understands. We hope and expect that this means the child's behaviour will change after this. For children with serious behavioural problems, this is usually not the case. As the adult, you can undermine your own plan in this way. After a "nice talk" you may feel pleased about your ability to reach the child after all, and convince him of how reasonable your arguments are. "See how easy it is!" You may even be persuaded to suspend the behaviour programme in the pro-active phase. This will leave you happily waiting in vain for the promised change in the child's behaviour. This is comparable to a football trainer having a "good talk" with a player and then concluding that training is no longer necessary.

The work session is the first part of the programme in which the child is involved. The phase in which you have said what you mean is followed by another important phase. You now have to mean what you say. If you leave it at saying what you are going to do, the child will soon catch on. Even a small child realises when his parents are making empty threats. The child will understand that he is in control, no matter what you say you are going to do, and will have no incentive to change his behaviour. You quickly lose your credibility as a coach if you say things but do not follow through. It demonstrates your powerlessness, and causes you to lose control and your position in the hierarchy. As a result, the educational situation continues to be a power struggle. "Saying what you mean and meaning what you say" is about being consistent and staying in control. But its full impact can only be achieved in combination with growth-promoting language used in the context of a coaching model.

This chapter was about holding a pro-active work session. In the next chapter you will implement the sanction you announced, during the reactive part of the intervention.

4. HOLD A WORK SESSION USING GROWTH-PROMOTING LANGUAGE

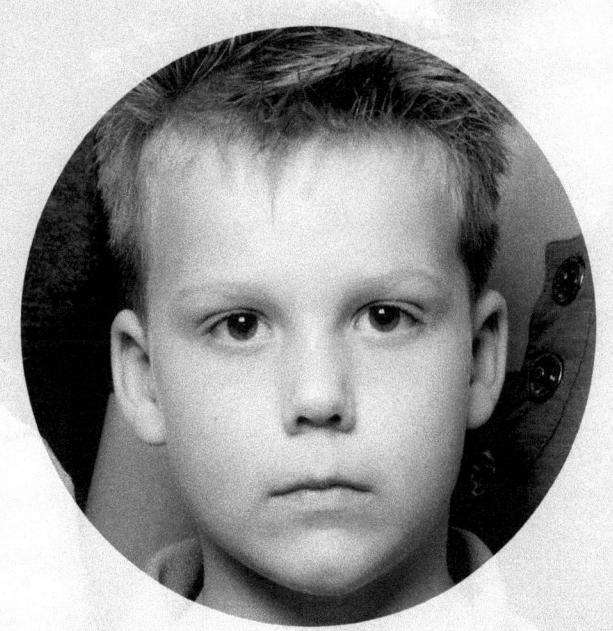

5. Apply the sanction

5. APPLY THE SANCTION

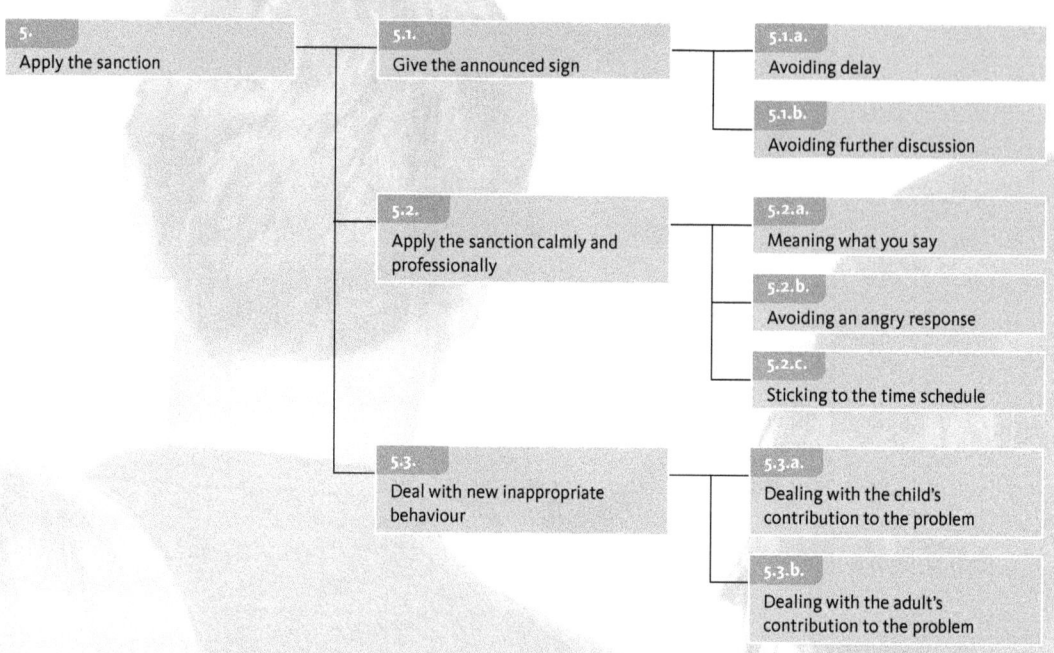

- **5.** Apply the sanction
  - **5.1.** Give the announced sign
    - **5.1.a.** Avoiding delay
    - **5.1.b.** Avoiding further discussion
  - **5.2.** Apply the sanction calmly and professionally
    - **5.2.a.** Meaning what you say
    - **5.2.b.** Avoiding an angry response
    - **5.2.c.** Sticking to the time schedule
  - **5.3.** Deal with new inappropriate behaviour
    - **5.3.a.** Dealing with the child's contribution to the problem
    - **5.3.b.** Dealing with the adult's contribution to the problem

What is this chapter about?

Say what you mean and mean what you say. You no longer have to be afraid of the moment when the inappropriate behaviour occurs. You have repaired your work attitude and devised and announced an intervention. Now all parties know what is going to happen. This chapter helps you to apply the sanction during the reactive moment.

5. Apply the sanction

Portrait of a younger child
"Shouting at the table"

We met Jill, the mother of Josh (six), Amy (five) and Paul (two) in chapter 1. Jill has decided that she wants to do something about Josh's behaviour. Her husband has reluctantly agreed to this. Together they read the section on repairing their work attitude. Then they each make a list of Josh's inappropriate behaviour. Because the situation during meals is high on both lists they decide to start there. During meals Josh exhibits different kinds of inappropriate behaviour but his parents want to start with his shouting. His screams are blood curdling. The parents invite Josh to a work session on Sunday afternoon. Josh thinks this is exciting and interesting. For once he is not being scolded. His parents even say he is too big now for them to follow him around policing his behaviour. They tell him that they know that everyone in the family wants to enjoy mealtimes. And that they are going to help Josh practice this. The plan is as follows: the first time Josh shouts at the table, he will get a yellow card. If he shouts again during the meal, he will be sent into the hall for five minutes. When his time is up his mother or father will come and get him. If he shouts again during the meal, he will be sent back to the hall again.

Portrait of an older child
"Child's attempts to destabilise the situation"

A behaviour programme is needed for Robert. He lived with his father for a time but now he is living with his mother again. His mother works almost full-time and she is intensely irritated by the fact that Robert does virtually nothing all day. When she comes home from work, Robert is looking intently at his computer. It looks as if he went straight from his bed onto the internet. His breakfast dishes have not been cleared away. She is sick and tired of the fact that every time she asks him to do something, he says "Yeah, in a minute…" He subsequently does nothing at all, and that makes her even more frustrated.

Introduction

The *reactive* moment is the moment when the incident takes place. Before you started this programme, the reactive moment was horrible. Now it gives you the opportunity to scale back the child's inappropriate behaviour. Preparing for it makes the reactive moment less fraught, because partial interventions take place before and after this moment. You now know that the inappropriate behaviour will probably occur, and both you and the child know what will happen when it does. At this point it is important to do exactly what you have said you will do. You give the announced warning, and if necessary you apply the announced sanction. As with every form of training, consistent repetition is an important part of this programme. You are prepared for the child's attempts to disrupt the programme. And even for your own attempts to cut corners during training.

5.1. Give the announced sign

Portrait of a younger child

When the family sits down at the table, Jill reminds her son of their agreement. Josh remembers. After awhile Amy drops her spoon on the floor, and pushes her chair back to look for it. Josh shouts very loudly: "Hey! You're not supposed to get up while we're eating!" Jill says to Josh: "That's what we were talking about Josh. Now you are getting a yellow card." Josh is angry. He says, "It's not fair! Amy is not supposed to get up while we're eating!" Jill calmly says: "We are practicing not shouting. We are doing it the way we agreed." She then shows him the yellow card.

Portrait of an older child

It is definitely time for a plan. Robert's mother is familiar with the programme, which she also used for an older son who now lives on his own. She tells Robert that she cannot cope with how he chooses to live. He is more than welcome to live with her, but it is not a hotel, and she is not a maid (brief reason). She thinks that he is too old to have her following him around like a police officer (growth-promoting language). She has made a list of the chores she expects Robert to do every day or every week. She is no longer going to nag him about them, but they will have a weekly work session (process box, announcing the intervention). After a month she will determine whether or not it works. Robert does his chores for a few days, then he slacks off. His mother says nothing, because the first work session is not until four days later.

Now give the warning sign you said you would give. Do not postpone the intervention and do not discuss the matter any longer.

5.1.a. Avoiding delay

Do the following:
- If the relevant inappropriate behaviour occurs, give the agreed sign immediately (yellow card, raised index finger, etc.)
- Do this calmly, but firmly.
- Be prepared for the child's attempts to delay the process.
- Stick to the time limit you have set for the child to stop the inappropriate behaviour.

5.1.b. Avoiding further discussion

Do the following:
- Be aware of the fact that the intervention starts now.
- Do not hold any further content arguments with the child, even though you and/or the child were accustomed to arguing this point.
- From now on, either party's attempt to do so should be regarded as an avoidant tactic.
- Do not let yourself be drawn into a discussion, but say a sentence such as: "Now we are doing what we agreed to do."

> **Consider the following:**

Ensure that the sanction is not postponed. The child will interpret postponement as an opportunity to continue the inappropriate behaviour. What the child sees is that **you say what you mean, but do not mean what you say**. Remember that at this point every discussion or explanation is a form of postponement. All participants already know what is going to happen when the inappropriate behaviour occurs. It has been clearly announced in advance and there is no need for further discussion.

From now on, you will be working on the inappropriate behaviour. Content discussions will not take place until the behaviour no longer occurs. Any discussion during this phase is about training, and does not take place until the post-active part of the intervention. A discussion should never lead to a further avoidance of intervening in the inappropriate behaviour.

It is counter-productive to hold a discussion in this phase, because it would always be about the child's excuses. The child wants to explain why he could not hold up his end of the bargain this time, or why it was not his fault. The discussion would also inevitably be about the disappointment that you, the adult, experience every time the child fails to hold up his end of the bargain. And then it would be about how the child promises again and again to hold up his end of the bargain. Or about the child's refusal to keep any kind of a promise at all. These are futile "discussions", and the time for them has passed. You now do what you said you would do: you give the agreed sign.

The child may try to throw you off balance. For example, by suggesting that this was not what you had agreed, that you said something else and therefore it is unfair. The child may vehemently protest that there is no way he intends to participate in such an unfair decision. The child may also maintain that he did not understand what you meant. It should be clear, however, that there is just one criterion for not imposing the sanction: that can happen only if the child has stopped the inappropriate behaviour.

5.2. Apply the sanction calmly and professionally

> **Portrait of a younger child**
>
> *Josh is temporarily taken aback by the yellow card. He calms down and carries on eating. But he continues to give Amy angry looks. When Amy spreads jam from an almost empty pot onto her bread, Josh shouts: "Hey, you can't have all the jam!" His mother calmly gets up and tells Josh that this is what they are practicing. She accompanies him to the hall and says he can sit on the stairs. She will come and get him after five minutes. The door is closed and the family continues eating. They hear Josh moving around in the hall and hear him say that he thinks this is "stupid". After a few minutes everything is quiet, and Josh is welcomed back to the table after exactly five minutes. A little later, when Josh loudly protests another perceived injustice, he gets another yellow card, and soon after that his mother brings him to the hall again. When he has been there for two minutes he opens the door and asks if the five minutes are up. His mother says that she will come and get him when the time is up. She adds: "And Josh, we are going to practice this too. If you come in again before your time is up, another five minutes will be added."*

Portrait of an older child

We saw that Robert does his chores for only a few days. After that he slacks off. His mother says nothing, because the time is still running in the process box (read the explanation of the process box on page 109, Appendix B). She sees what's happening but waits until the first work session to discuss it. She does not nag Robert or remind him of his chores. She sticks to her part of the bargain and does what she says she would do. This means she takes Robert seriously. She regards him as an adolescent who is capable of holding up his end of a bargain. While time is running in the process box, she is not angry, sarcastic or ironic. It is a training process and making denigrating remarks to the child you are training is not helpful. Robert has the opportunity to be autonomous within certain time limits. He is also given freedom at home within certain limits. His mother is treating him according to the age at which he claims to function. Robert's mother also sticks to the time schedule; the first work session is not for four days. Yet Robert feels a bit uneasy.

Now apply the sanction calmly and professionally. Do exactly what you pro-actively announced you would do. Do not be angry but be very exact about the time.

5.2.a. Meaning what you say

Do the following:
- Apply the sanction in a calm, professional manner if the child has not responded to the sign or if the child has responded only temporarily.
- Do exactly what you have said you would do, no more or less.
- Do not postpone the sanction.
- Repeat the sanction often if necessary
- Avoid escalations.

5.2.b. Avoiding an angry response

Do the following:
- Try not to show your anger when imposing the sanction; keep your attitude neutral and friendly.
- Behave like a trainer, not someone meting out punishment
- Do not expect the child to understand that you mean well.
- Do not let the child's reaction make you angry,
- If the behaviour quickly repeats itself, do not be disappointed. Repeat the intervention.
- See the recurring behaviour as an opportunity to practice.

5.2.c. Sticking to the time schedule

Do the following:
- Be scrupulous about respecting the time schedule when applying the sanction.
- Do not use time as a means of increasing the severity of the sanction.
- Realise that success depends on the consistent repetition of a smaller sanction.
- If the behaviour does not improve, repeat the sanction but stick to the time schedule.

Consider the following:

The inappropriate behaviour takes place in the reactive moment. In the past this moment often led to an escalation. Again and again, the inappropriate behaviour took you by surprise and pinned you down in the reactive moment. Your only choice was to react to something you had hoped would not happen again. But you were a step behind every time, and the vicious circle of anger, disappointment, powerlessness and rage started again.

Now the reactive moment has been unburdened because everyone knows what will happen if the inappropriate behaviour occurs. This is more pleasant, and safer, for both you and the child. This is the moment when the change in the educational situation becomes visible. That is why it is important that you actually apply the relevant sanction. Now is not the time for doubt, and certainly not the time to quit. The child must not be given the chance to sidestep the consequences. The combination of **"saying what you mean and meaning what you say"** shows the child that you are active, consistent and fair. The sanctions no longer resemble an unannounced explosion. Nor are sanctions announced and subsequently postponed or altered. There is now a programme in place which was announced to the child in advance, and which is aimed at training and development.

Although your own course of action is now clear, you may still have to improvise now and then. This can happen if the child is physically stronger than you are. The consistent application of the sanction could then lead to an escalation. You may also find yourself outnumbered by children or young people during an escalation at home, in the classroom or on the street, and lacking support from other adults. This does not mean that you have to get caught up in a power struggle. The sanction can be assigned exactly as announced. However, you improvise by indicating that the sanction will be carried out at some other moment. When designing the intervention you need to take the situation surrounding its application into account. If application is not feasible, the sanction will be changed the next time. This too should be discussed with the child. Give yourself time to deal with such situations. This will help you to avoid using disappointment about the application of the intervention as an excuse for a passive work attitude.

Remember that you, the adult, no longer have to be angry: you have designed a project aimed at scaling back inappropriate behaviour. You are not going to use anger as a strategy because you have realised that it no longer helps. You are prepared because you now assume that the child will display the inappropriate behaviour. You have devised an intervention in advance and everyone knows what is going to happen. Although you are resolute, you are now able to carry out the intervention in a friendly manner. It is the friendliness of a trainer.

However, the child may be so unreachable that you become angry anyway. He may say "I couldn't care less about the sanction" or "Do whatever you like…" or "You know what you can do with your sanction…" You can respond by saying "It's alright for you not to care, but we are doing what we agreed to do", or "I understand that this is no fun for you, but we are going to do what was agreed".

A time-out situation requires exact timing on the part of the adult. If the time out is five minutes, do not cut corners. Short time outs may result in the child being sent away several times during a meal, or sent out of the classroom several times during a lesson. You can keep a record of these short time outs and compare them for use during the post-active phase during which you discuss the training.

Remember that the length of the sanction does not determine whether or not it works. It is about meaning what you say and repeating it consistently during the training programme. If for example a child is not allowed to ride his bike for three weeks because he refused to put it away, the child will learn nothing new from the sanction after the first few days. But if you consistently repeat a short sanction, the child learns more about cause and effect, and his own role in that process. Every time he fails to store his bicycle properly he will lose 15 minutes of television time. Even if his favourite programme is on. The immediacy of the sanction highlights the connection between the action and the actor. In addition, it is simply easier to practice if the child has his bicycle.

Initially, repeating the sanction will remind the adult of the bad times before the intervention. That is why it is important to remember that sanctions will have to be repeated. That is what training is. The fact that you take the time to repeat the sanction tells the child that you take the matter seriously. It shows that you think practicing with him is worthwhile. This is something not often experienced by children with behavioural problems.

Being aware that this is a training process is also good for you. It gives you an opportunity to take the angry, sometimes sarcastic, tone out of your sanctions. With practice you learn how to apply the sanctions calmly and consistently.

5.3. Deal with new inappropriate behaviour

Portrait of a younger child

It is an unusual meal for Josh. He has already been sent to the hall twice. He thinks this is unfair. He's not allowed to say anything! He is especially angry at Amy. She also does all kinds of things that aren't allowed, but she gets to stay at the table. Stupid sister! During the meal Josh gets a third time out. Just before he gets up Amy sticks out her tongue. Josh kicks her hard under the table. The mother responds immediately. She says she will talk to Amy later. She tells Josh: "I see how angry you are, Josh, but you're not allowed to kick Amy. You have to stay out in the hall for seven minutes." Josh feels betrayed and he mumbles to his mother: "I don't care anyway!" His mother says: "I'm glad you don't care, but this is how it's going to be." Once Josh is in the hall, she explains to Amy that Josh has to practice sitting quietly at the table. She asks Amy to help by not making Josh angrier. Amy agrees to help. Her mother knows that Amy functions at an age-appropriate level. That is why she can have a conversation with her five-year old daughter. At this point, no programme is required.

Portrait of an older child

Robert initiates a conversation with his mother. He wants her to know he thinks he is being asked to do too much. He doesn't even have time to look into a study programme for next year. Wasn't that what his mother wanted him to do? His mother says she does not want to talk about this until their work session on Sunday. Now Robert is angry. "You just don't want to hear what I have to say." His mother replies, "I think what you have to say is very important. But that doesn't mean there are no rules. I have to stick to the rules because it's my duty to give you a proper upbringing." She stands firm and indicates that they will not discuss this until Sunday. Robert makes a show of being offended by her intransigence.

In this portrait we see an older child trying to destabilise the adult during the first few days of the programme. He does so by trying to start a conversation about substantive matters. The mother chooses the procedural approach: the programme train is now in motion and the next talking station is four days away. The mother remains in control and this makes Robert angry. Taking back control is Robert's objective. Doing so would give him the opportunity to continue the inappropriate behaviour, i.e. doing nothing. He tries another move, one that plays on her maternal feelings of guilt. Or on her desire to see him finally do something useful. When that too fails to get a response from her he pulls out all the stops: "This is so uncool! What a bitch you are!" His mother doesn't turn a hair.

By standing her ground, Robert's mother is doing more than he accuses her of doing. She is setting her boundaries as the mother of a family she has to manage on her own. She is setting up a content box (See page 109, Appendix B) by defining how much leeway he has in her house. She also sets up a process box (See page 109, Appendix B) by unilaterally deciding not to nag about household chores for a whole week. You might be tempted to think this is exactly what he wants. She is in a strong position now, and her attitude gives her leverage with Robert because it challenges him to become more active and take charge of his own development. Robert quickly gives up on his chores and also notices that he is no longer in control. His efforts to provoke his mother into arguing, and her refusal to do so, give her even more leverage. If he fails to do his chores in the days leading up to the work session he proves himself to be a younger, less independent child. His mother's position in this chess game becomes stronger. That is why it is so important for adults not to allow themselves to be drawn into content arguments once the programme is in place. All of the child's efforts should be regarded as additional inappropriate behaviour, and dealt with in a firm, friendly manner.

Check carefully now to determine whether you or the child are displaying additional inappropriate behaviour. This behaviour could still undermine the implementation of the programme.

5.3.a. Dealing with the child's contribution to the problem

Do the following:
- Keep in mind that additional inappropriate behaviour may take the form of the child's refusal to accept a time-out situation.
- Keep in mind that the sanction can make the child very angry.
- Keep in mind that the child may want to continue arguing.
- Keep in mind that the child can display a different form of inappropriate behaviour and claim that it is allowed because it was not included in the original definition.

- Make a distinction between this new behaviour and the behaviour you are training.
- Turn the reactive moment into a pro-active one by acknowledging the new behaviour and announcing what you plan to do if it has not stopped within a given time limit. Say for example: "I see how angry this makes you. You have five minutes to stop. If it doesn't, a new sanction will be added." Or: "You can moan about this for five minutes and then I'll give you a sign. If it doesn't stop then, a new sanction will follow."
- Think about the possibility of a reverse time out for older children. This involves removing yourself from the child's company, or stopping what you were doing (for instance helping the child with homework, waking him up, or making a meal) (See page 107, Appendix B).
- Try to anticipate the additional inappropriate behaviour, and incorporate this into the intervention. You can announce this in the next work session. For example say: "You may get very angry when the sanction is applied. In that case you can expect me to do the following."

5.3.b. Dealing with the adult's contribution to the problem

Do the following:
- Keep in mind that you can also show additional inappropriate behaviour. You may get angry during the intervention, forget to speak growth-promoting language or do something else that reflects a lack of experience or insufficient motivation.
- Remember that sometimes it just isn't your day (See page 103, Appendix A).
- If you notice that you are arguing again, stop the intervention abruptly and say to the child: "Okay, now I'm doing it myself. That was not what we agreed. I'm taking a minute's breather and then we will continue as agreed."
- Realise that the child may interpret this as a sign of weakness and an opportunity to take control again. He might say that he does not have to participate anymore. You confirm that it was not what you had agreed, but say, "we are starting over now". You take control again and continue as planned with the intervention.
- Keep in mind that you may start to think the planned intervention is too strict or too hard on the child. You may even be afraid of the child's anger and threats. It may be difficult for you to adopt an active work attitude.
- Realise that this could lead to additional inappropriate behaviour on your part, which could undermine the intervention.
- Remember that repeating steps 1 and 2 of the programme can help you to determine why the intervention has stalled.

Consider the following:
During the reactive moment the child may try to avoid the intervention. He may get angry and deliberately use additional inappropriate behaviour to undermine the intervention. This may affect your own motivation, particularly if you are already exhausted by your previous efforts to get a grip on the child's behaviour. It helps to understand that the problems are chronic, and that it will take time before the child is willing to cooperate and you start to see results. Try to adopt or regain an active work attitude. If necessary, read the first two chapters of this book again. You will not be defeated by the new inappropriate behaviour. Simply standing your ground will strengthen your position.

You can even take it one step further. It actually helps to assume that the child will have a negative response to the announcement or implementation of an intervention. You can regard this is an inevitable response. And this inevitable response then simply becomes the next step in the programme. It gives you the opportunity to respond in a neutral, somewhat cheerful fashion instead of with anger. During the reactive moment you can say: "It's a good thing this came up now; we can practice this too." You can include the "correction" in the programme in a positive way, with a thank-you.

It is a good idea to keep this in mind when you are devising the intervention. You can then take a pro-active stance and incorporate the negative version into the intervention. During the next work session you can say to the child: "You may want to talk a lot while the sanction is being carried out. I'm telling you now that I won't be responding to that." Or: "You may become very angry while the sanction is being carried and start hitting. If you do, this is what you can expect from me." Or: "When the sanction starts you may feel that you are being treated unfairly. I'm telling you now that I am not going to discuss it. Talking will come later." In this way the feared negative response can simply be built into the intervention and announced proactively.

We saw how the child tried to avoid the sanction. But you can be guilty of that as well. As the adult you may sincerely question whether the programme will work. But fear of the child's reaction can also be demotivating and obstructive. A classic question is: "And what if he won't do it?" Another frequently heard comment is: "Oh but that will make him really angry!" Fearing the reactions of others or your partner or ex-partner may also prevent you from carrying out the sanction. You may then convince yourself that this kind of programme does not work for this type of problem. And you will in fact be right: if you don't do it, it can't work.

As the adult you may also have a tendency to preach or to extract "good talks" from the child. Or to start explaining or arguing again. Think about a trainer trying to have a substantive talk with an athlete during a training session. You may do this more or less unconsciously. For example, in order to tone down the harshness of the intervention. Fear, guilt, or sympathy for the child can also play a role. However, dealing with substantive matters at this stage of the intervention will undermine your actions. Becoming angry has the same effect. If the child is able to provoke an angry response he is back in control. This should all be regarded as additional inappropriate behaviour on your part, because it encourages you to stop the planned intervention and revert to old behaviour patterns. The child will be only too glad to let this happen, or may even encourage it. If the training is interrupted the child has an opportunity to take control again.

This chapter discussed the reactive sanction. After pro-actively announcing what you were going to do if the inappropriate behaviour occurred, you reacted and did what you said you would do.

The sixth chapter and last part of the programme deals with the post-active part of the intervention. It involves discussing the training, and making growth-promoting comments about the child's efforts to control himself.

5. APPLY THE SANCTION

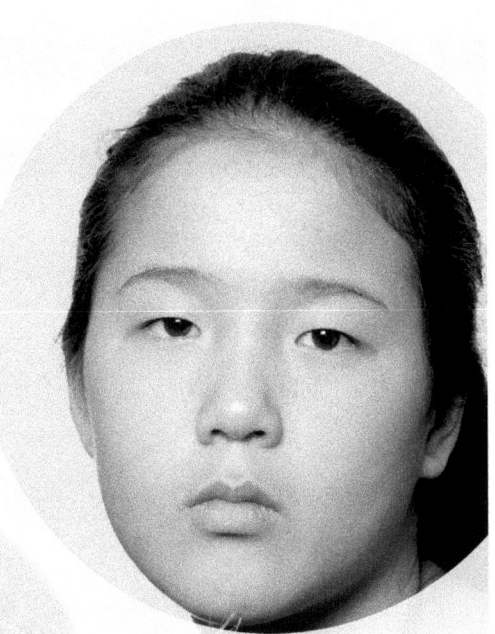

6. Use growth-promoting language to evaluate the intervention

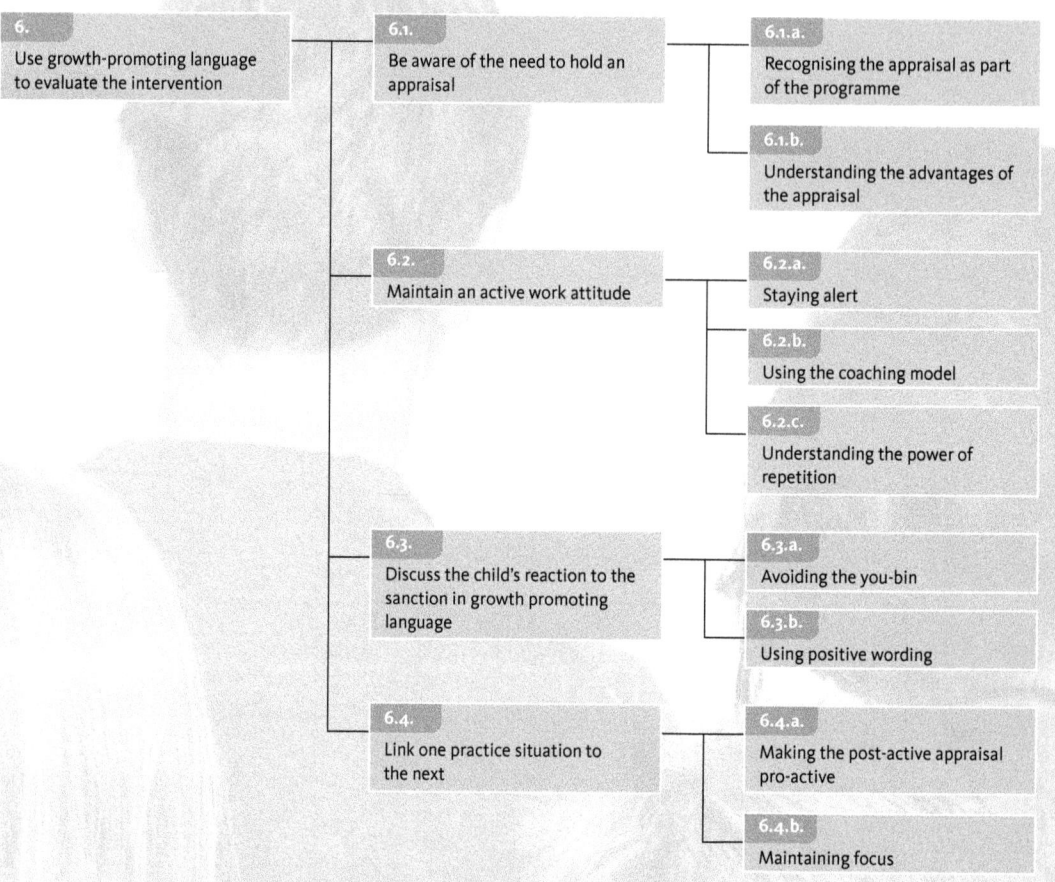

What is this chapter about?

A short appraisal is part of the programme. You regard the entire intervention as practice for the child, and discuss this practice in growth-promoting language. The child gradually learns to connect his behaviour to its consequences. This encourages him to make a habit of showing a different kind of behaviour. This chapter helps you to carry out your appraisal.

6. Use growth-promoting language to evaluate the intervention

Portrait of a younger child
"Shouting at the table"

Jill, whom we met in chapters 1 and 5, is following a programme with Josh (six years) designed to scale back inappropriate behaviour: shouting during meals. Her husband is also participating. They have held a pro-active work session. The reactive step is to give Josh a yellow card, and if he shouts after that he gets a five-minute time out. The post-active step involves welcoming Josh back to the table in growth-promoting language.

Portrait of an older child
"Whatever... I'm going out"

Final exams are two months away. Matthew's parents have the impression that he has done little to prepare. His father has advised him not to go out on Friday and Saturday night but he thinks this is ridiculous. As if that would work! On Saturday! Saturday is for sleeping in after a hard week at school, sports, and then a night out with friends. And Sunday? Sunday's no good at all. Sunday is for watching a game with a take away meal, not for studying. Isn't it? But work? What was it his father called it? Working ahead! He really doesn't get it. Everyone knows that maths is nothing more than doing a few sums. You're alright as long as you do that. And he just needs to get a few summaries off the internet for his reading list. They're all there on line. The old man can really go on about things! Nobody actually reads those books, do they? As far as he is concerned, he's is going out on Saturday night. Besides he's already made arrangements and promised his friends he'd come.

Matthew's father makes it very clear that he disagrees. He argues that these are the only few weeks in Matthew's entire school career that he really needs to work hard. It's crunch time! He needs to show some character and buckle down, and not just squeak by with mediocre grades. His results so far have not been all that good. Matthew makes a half-hearted attempt to convince his father that he is wrong. When his father subsequently makes another attempt to persuade Matthew of the importance of doing his best, Matthew cuts him off with "Yeah Dad, in your day everything was better and everyone got perfect results." His father realises that further discussion is useless. He can't think of anything better to say than "I just don't want you to go." To which Matthew simply replies: "Whatever, I'm going out".

Introduction

The appraisal introduces the idea that you can practice something, and then talk about it or think about it afterwards. For a child with behavioural problems, this is not an obvious conclusion. He is used to staying well away from any involvement. In the post-active phase you have the opportunity to change this situation, and adopt a coaching role. Even if you have argued with the child throughout the day, you can sit down on his bed in the evening and say: "We certainly argued a lot today, didn't we? We'll start over tomorrow. Sleep tight." It only takes a few short sentences. You invite the child to think about the day's arguments and about your changed attitude at this moment. This can also work at school. The message to the child is that this is possible too. However, do not become over-optimistic about the possibility of having a good talk with the child.

The pro-active phase of the intervention dealt with re-establishing the hierarchy. The reactive phase involved being consistent in a calm manner. The post-active phase is about teaching the child to think about his own behaviour. The objective is to keep both you and the child on your toes for the next part of the programme. Now that you have taken the reins you need to stay in charge.

6.1. Be aware of the need to hold an appraisal

Portrait of a younger child

After every time out, Josh's mother welcomes him back with growth-promoting language. The father says nothing at the table, but later he tells his wife he thinks it is all a bit over the top: "He's just going to have to learn to behave himself. What good does it do to pamper him after he's been punished?" The mother understands why this is necessary, but has trouble expressing this. Josh's behavioural therapist explains it to them again. "Josh does have to learn to behave himself. But don't forget that he has just started the programme. He is still functioning at a low level. Don't apply a standard that belongs to a higher level. Try to find his actual level. Talk about training instead of punishment." The behavioural therapist explains to Josh's parents that the pro-active part of the intervention is used to reinstate the hierarchy in the educational situation. The objective of the post-active phase is to stimulate the child to think about his behaviour. You do this by being consistent and by talking about training using growth-promoting language. The father agrees to try this.

Portrait of an older child

Matthew's father understands that he is in a difficult educational position. Whatever he does now, there is a risk involved. If he constantly nags Matthew, or punishes him too harshly, Matthew will balk. If he does nothing, Matthew will make a mess of things. What can he do? He maps out the situation once again. Then he fixes his own work attitude, which in this case means accepting that Matthew will probably not pass his exams. This gives him a bit of breathing space. In a pro-active work session he tells Matthew that he doesn't want to follow him around nagging. At the same time he calmly but very clearly states that he is adamantly opposed to Matthew's behaviour. He briefly tells him what he considers to be inappropriate behaviour: doing nothing about his exam and going out once or twice at the weekend.

The intervention is simple. Every time Matthew displays this behaviour, his parents will do nothing to stop him. But he will be excluded from participation, just like an athlete who fails to respect the rules of the game. His parents are assuming that Matthew has no interest in the family's activities. If he comes home too late, the door will be locked with a latch. His parents will lock up when they go to bed. If Matthew is late for dinner without notice, he will have to fend for himself. The home restaurant will be closed. These are harsh and ostensibly cold measures. However, they mean that Matthew is being taken seriously and his actions mirrored.

After two weeks the father has a work session with Matthew to find out how things are going. There are no visible signs that Matthew has done anything about his exams. He has gone out five times in two weeks and has noticed that his parents mean what they say. Matthew finds his father in a cheerful mood, which he thinks is odd. He must know that Matthew has spent the last two weeks partying and smoking cannabis. Have they stopped caring about him?

Remember that appraisal is an essential part of the programme. It gives the child a tool to help him think about his own behaviour.

6.1.a. Recognising the appraisal as part of the programme

Do the following:
- Always conduct an appraisal of the relevant behaviour or of how the child responded to the sanction.
- Never omit this step because it highlights the child's training results at every level of functioning. You show the child your appreciation by redefining the intervention as difficult but good practice.
- A brief comment about how things went can also be regarded as an appraisal.
- Do this when the child is alone and when there is no escalation.
- Take the initiative and persevere even if the child "doesn't feel like it" or is recalcitrant.
- Do not lecture at this point.
- Do not force the child into a content dispute.

6.1.b. Understanding the advantages of the appraisal

Do the following:
- Keep in mind that an appraisal gradually teaches the child to think about his own behaviour. With each intervention, his behaviour will develop if his efforts to get that behaviour under control are appreciated.
- See his reaction to a sanction or to the entire intervention as an active attempt to do so. Even if the child has shown a lot of resistance and strict limits have had to be enforced.
- Keep in mind that an appraisal reinforces your role as a coach in a growth-promoting model. Even if you have to intervene often and forcefully, the objective of this strategy is to develop less inappropriate behaviour.
- The appraisal should therefore be regarded as a second work session with a child in training.

Consider the following:
The purpose of a preliminary discussion is to announce the training session, and the purpose of an appraisal is to review that session. The appraisal is an important part of the programme. It should not be omitted "because things are going better now". Or because "he won't do it anyway". And especially not because "behaving appropriately is normal". An appraisal is about the sanction and the child's response to it. It is an appraisal of a training session. Keep in mind that the programme is designed to unburden the reactive moment by making good use of the pro-active and post-active moments. The post-active work session can be very brief.

An appraisal can also serve as the conclusion of one part of the programme, and the announcement of another part. This happens when the inappropriate behaviour has improved to an acceptable level and you are ready to move on to the next point on the list. You can now announce that a new work session will soon be held. Both the conclusion and the announcement should be made in growth-promoting language. "It's going so well that we can start on the next subject." For teenagers, the language can be geared to their age level: "That was a lot faster than I expected. We're ready for the next step."

You may wonder why an appraisal is necessary. The child may find it difficult or impossible to reflect on his behaviour during such an appraisal. What purpose does it serve? The appraisal is important because it gives the child recognition for practicing. It benefits the child in the following ways:

1. You discuss how the practice session went. This gives the child one more opportunity to think about what he was practicing, and stimulates the child's ability to familiarise himself with it.
2. The child learns that it is apparently possible to practice something, and that what you have practiced then becomes part of you.
3. Consistently referring to the child's behaviour and the sanction as "practicing" has an important function. Punishment is replaced by training. The child is challenged to develop new behaviour.
4. There is a time effect. You refer to "practicing" during every appraisal. In time the child will recognise this as a project. A project that he can influence. It is the training and the effort to achieve something that are important.

This is a remarkable challenge for an angry, unmotivated child. He has no intention of giving up his power. However, the intervention caused by his bad behaviour is consistently referred to as training or practicing on his behaviour. The challenge lies in the uncertainty that this generates. The child had assumed that his behaviour put him in control. The introduction of words such as training and practicing make it clear that this is a game he has yet to learn. The child will be asking himself how he can take back control. The answer turns out to be: by developing himself. Gradually, the child realises that he can have more control if he shows less inappropriate behaviour.

For a child who has been participating in this game for awhile, the term "practicing on your behaviour" is also a challenge. At the very least the child will have discovered that less inappropriate behaviour results in fewer sanctions. It is also possible for a child to see real growth as a challenge. Especially if he has noticed that family or group relationships have improved. That is a lot more fun than sanctions. There is apparently a connection between the improvement and the child's behaviour. The child may even start to enjoy the programme, and progress from scaling back inappropriate behaviour to developing appropriate behaviour.

6.2. Maintain an active work attitude

Portrait of a younger child

During the first week of the behavioural programme Josh gets an average of six time outs every meal. That is tiring for both the parents and Josh. However, Josh's mother understands that it was even more tiring before they started the programme. Then she was exhausted before the meal began, hoping that this time it wouldn't be disrupted. Just this once. Now they have a whole programme to follow but at least they are working on the problem. If things go badly one day, she can still muster the energy to go to Josh after his father has put him to bed. She says: "I know it was still hard for you to practice today. We'll start again tomorrow " She gives him a big kiss.

> **Portrait of an older child**
> During the work session Matthew's father asks how things went. Matthew says: "Alright." His father simply says: "I know how things went. Do you want me to help you or do you want to do it on your own?" Matthew maintains that he can do it on his own, and that he has more than enough time. His father says: "Great. I'll ask you again in precisely one week's time. In the meantime we'll just carry on".

Maintain an active work attitude and be alert to any recurrence of the inappropriate behaviour you are practicing on. Be prepared to repeat interventions. Act as a coach so that the intervention becomes and remains a training session.

6.2.a. Staying alert

Do the following:
- Ensure that you do not lose focus following an intervention.
- Ensure that you remain in an active position and do not relapse into passivity in the hope that things will better from now on.
- Keep in mind the child's inappropriate behaviour will soon recur. Your response has to be consistent with what you have pro-actively announced.
- Be prepared for the frequent repetition of the inappropriate behaviour.
- Be prepared for the content leak. Read about this in Appendix C, page 115 This refers to content arguments that keep you and other adults from sticking to the programme. This is adult behaviour that allows the child to continue the inappropriate behaviour.

6.2.b. Using the coaching model

Do the following
- Act as a coach and not as a passive judge.
- Stick to the chosen training model.
- Do not use the appraisal to vent your anger about the child's behaviour.
- Show an interest in what the child is practicing.
- Be empathetic when things go well. Be empathetic when they do not.
- Continue to emphasise that the child is practicing, but be very consistent when it comes to applying sanctions.

6.2.c. Understanding the power of repetition

Do the following:
- Be prepared to repeat the programme, now and when you are scaling back other behaviour. This is a training programme for both the child and you, the adult.
- Do not give up if you do not see immediate results.
- Do not give up if you are having trouble with the "perfect" execution of the programme.
- See the necessity of repetition as an opportunity for improvement.

Consider the following:

You are now working on the sixth and final step of the programme. You have placed yourself in an active position, and introduced a game in which you also participate. This game requires your active attention. There will definitely be a further round of inappropriate behaviour so it is important to remain alert. There is no need to waste energy hoping that the behaviour will not recur. This is not a one-off intervention, after which you can passively sink back into a comfortable chair. That would only lead to further disappointment, desperation and loss of control. Keep in mind that it is in the child's interests to try to take back or remain in control. Your desperation and disappointment are to his advantage. Try to think of yourself as a carriage driver with a team of horses. You have to learn how to follow a consistent course, but also to remain flexible in your response to the horses' actions.

A short appraisal confirms that you have taken the lead. You are the one who determines when the appraisal will take place. If you do that in coaching way, you also reaffirm the training model you have introduced. This is possible even in situations that are still difficult to manage. Understand that coaching is about how you approach the child and evaluating what he is capable of at this moment.

For a child with a long-standing behavioural problem, developing more appropriate behaviour is an extraordinary peak performance. Do not be tempted to regard more appropriate behaviour as the obvious outcome of a lengthy practice period. Or to forget that for this child, this is a major step. Always reminding the child what his "normal" level of behaviour should be is also passive and judgmental. Judging is not coaching; it is leaving the child to his devices.

The strength of this programme lies in consistent repetition. Repetition teaches the child that the programme is actually being applied. And repetition gives you the opportunity to announce your strategy proactively, and to follow it in a consistent manner. You learn how to say what you mean and mean what you say, and to do so using coaching, growth-promoting language. It takes practice to learn to see this programme as a game. Practice takes time. You felt angry, powerless and sad when you faced up to the need to work with this programme. It takes some time before you can feel like you are back in the saddle again, and in control.

Practice actively, but do not judge what you have achieved so far too harshly. Remember that no matter how active your work attitude, you cannot practice everything at once. It helps to remember that you are no longer a passive bystander but an active participant. Repetition of the programme is practice for the trainer.

Keep in mind that the child is also practicing showing more appropriate behaviour. His practicing is not voluntary. The child has to give up previously acquired power over the educational situation. That power enabled the child to manipulate others without much effort. If the sanctions are consistently applied, the child's first reaction is to make the best of a bad bargain, which is not at all the same thing as voluntarily displaying more appropriate behaviour. It will take some time for the child to become interested in growth, and in displaying and being rewarded for better behaviour. Here too, repetition is practice .

6.3. Discuss the child's reaction to the sanction in growth-promoting language

Portrait of a younger child

The programme is in its fourth week. Josh is consistently given time outs if he shouts at the table. His mother comes to get him when he has spent five minutes in the hall. He is allowed to sit down at the table again. Because Josh was very quiet in the hall, his mother says: "I noticed the progress you've made and how quickly you calmed down in the hall, Josh. Great! Come back to the table." If Josh is later sent back to the hall for a second time, and is soon quiet, his mother says: "You've made more progress, Josh. Good job!" She keeps her comments brief, but never forgets to add a post-active comment in growth-promoting language. She consciously chooses this language, and consistently uses positive wording.

Portrait of an older child

Matthew's father has taken the initiative and ended the very short work session. Matthew does not like it. "Hey what's wrong old man? Am I in for some more punishment? Come on!" In a friendly tone his father says: "Think of me as a trainer. If the player doesn't want to train, the session is over. Let me know if you want to do something next week." He gets up and walks away. He hears Matthew say: "Wow, he really has lost it."

Now review the sanction with the child.

6.3.a. Avoiding the you-bin

Do the following:
- Avoid the you-bin (See page 116, Appendix C).
- Talk about how the training went.
- Keep in mind that a child functioning at a lower level has been scolded a lot.
- Keep in mind that encouraging words benefit the child more than confronting him with disappointing results.
- Be aware of how counter-productive the you-bin is. If behaviour has improved, comments such as "See, you can do it…" or "If only you could do that without my having to ask you four times" do not help the child.
- Do not use good results as the new norm.
- Comment on the training and not on the results.
- Discuss how difficult it was to practice, but say you saw how hard the child was trying.
- Emphasise the practicing aspect of a session that went well.

6.3.b. Using positive wording

Do the following:
- Speak growth-promoting language in the appraisal, using words that praise the child for how well the practice went. Read about growth-promoting language in Appendix C, page 113.
- If the response to the sanction was favourable or the child tried to practice, use a sentence that begins like this: "You're making progress. I saw how quickly you …"
- If the child did not respond well to the sanction, use a sentence that beings with "I saw how hard it still is for you…" This is encouraging in situations you have been practicing for a longer period.
- Realise that in both situations you are encouraging the child. If the child quickly calms down in the hall, you are indicating that it happened sooner than you expected, and that the child has made progress. If the child still finds it difficult to calm down, you are indicating that you expect an improvement soon.
- Keep in mind that this choice of words makes it possible to conduct the appraisal in growth-promoting language, even if the results were not that good.
- Try to make a habit of using these positive phrases.

Consider the following:
The purpose of a post-active appraisal is to discuss the effort, and not the results. What matters is that the child is practicing to get a better grip on his own behaviour. That is a difficult exercise for the child, and it is important to reward even small efforts with positive comments. The child has become accustomed to being scolded for his behaviour. The appraisal gives him the chance to hear something encouraging about every effort (regardless of whether it was prompted by a sanction) to change that behaviour. To encourage practice, your comments are made in growth-promoting language, avoiding the you-bin.

The above phrases will help you to use growth-promoting language during the appraisal. If, for example, a child has become calmer during a time out, you may want to compliment him when he returns to the table or the group: "Well done, come back in now". But you can also use growth-promoting language: "You're making progress. I saw how quickly you calmed down, come back in and we'll start again." Using the word **progress** has a leverage effect because it suggests that the child became calm more quickly than you, the adult, expected. This emphasises that this is something the child has achieved, not you. It also indicates that in spite of the difficult circumstances, the child is capable of growth.

You can also use growth-promoting language if the time out did not go very well. In this situation, using the word "still" creates leverage: "I see that you **still** had trouble staying calm in the hall, but you can come back inside now". The word "still" implies that you, the adult, are confident that in time the situation will improve. That is entirely different from comments such as: "You just don't learn, do you?" or "What a pity. We hoped it would go a bit better this time".

Growth-promoting language refers to the manner in which the child is approached during consistent action on the part of the adult. It is not about giving unmerited praise, or about continuing to tolerate inappropriate behaviour. Growth-promoting language and consistency are not mutually exclusive. It is important to realise, however, that consistent action needs to be based on a growth-promoting model, and not on a punishment model. Growth-promoting language encourages the child to practice more than punitive language would. You can use growth-promoting language as a post-active comment regardless the child's level of functioning.

It is language based on the concept of development, and development can start at any level. But it takes time and practice. Development may stagnate at some point, but your comments should always be formulated as growth-promoting language.

6.4. Link one practice situation to the next

Portrait of a younger child

Josh is welcomed back every time he returns to the table after a time out. But his parents have taught themselves to say that the sanction will be applied in exactly the same way the next time. They have even thought of a creative variation on this theme: "You have practiced so well that you know exactly what will happen next time." After a month or two Josh's parents take stock of the situation. Jill says in the first week Josh was given a time out roughly six times during every meal. In the second week, it was only twice during a meal. During the third and fourth week Josh proudly announced that he hadn't had a yellow card yet. The frequency of the time outs is now very low.

In this portrait we have seen shouting at the table change from being a recurring source of irritation into a well-functioning project. Both Josh and his parents have become accustomed to the intervention. As far as this "file" is concerned, the hierarchy has been restored. The intervention aimed at shouting has also meant that Josh behaves better at the table. The feedback is positive because it is much more pleasant to have a meal with him. After a few weeks Josh starts to enjoy exercising self-control, and not getting a yellow card. He is much less angry and even takes a little pride in hearing his parents say that he is ready for the next exercise.

Portrait of an older child

It has been two weeks since the first work session, and Matthew's participation in the second work session was not very positive either. He tried to badger his father by calling him a robot who was programmed to keep repeating the same text, but his father did not take the bait. After Matthew said that he didn't need any help, his father calmly concluded the work session. "Let's see what happens next week". Exams are just one month away. Matthew is intimidated by his father's change of attitude. He is interested but he does not get angry. Matthew is not very happy that the ball is always in his court now. Moreover, he is starting to get nervous about those stupid exams. He has also noticed that his friends Rowan and Justin did not go out on Saturday night. When his father makes a casual remark about next year's final exams, he explodes: "Come off it, you don't really think I'm not going to pass do you? No way, man." This is the only time that his father makes a content-based comment. "Well Matthew I think it's realistic to assume that you are not going to pass. It's hard to win any competition if you don't train." Matthew asks his father: "What are you going to do if I don't make it. Are you going to kick me out?" His father replies that Matthew would start with a clean slate, but that the house rules would be the same.

Now make the link to the next practice situation. This applies to both the child and the adult, and does not take much time. Both parties have to realise that the programme will continue, regardless of the results so far. During the appraisal of an intervention, the boundaries can be moved for the next round of the behavioural programme. Post-active becomes pro-active.

6.4.a. Making the post-active appraisal pro-active

Do the following:
- Use the appraisal as a preliminary discussion of what will happen if the inappropriate behaviour recurs.
- Use growth-promoting language during the appraisal but be very clear about what the child can expect the next time.
- Do that in an encouraging way. Show that you are interested in the next practice session.
- Do not expect the child to be happy about this or to help you plan it.
- Use the appraisal to announce small changes or additions.
- Use the appraisal as a link to the next pro-active work session. Indicate that tomorrow you will repeat what has been agreed one more time. You might say: "Tomorrow morning I will warn you when we are about to start." The child knows what to expect today and tomorrow.
- Conclude the post-active part of the intervention in a friendly tone by announcing that you will start again with a clean slate.
- However, make it clear that you will respond in the agreed manner every time. This applies even if the sanction has to be applied several times a day.

6.4.b. Maintaining focus

Do the following:
- Make sure you do not lose focus during the intervention. Do not carelessly let the programme slacken and gradually slip away.
- Keep in mind that the child will notice this immediately, and the educational system may gradually deteriorate.
- During the next round of the programme, do exactly what you told the child you would do.
- Hold a brief but precise discussion of how the intervention went. This emphasises your role as the child's coach and the person in charge of the behavioural programme.
- If you are unable to complete the programme, or if you have to interrupt it due to illness, hold a work session with the child to announce a temporary stop. Compare it to a training programme that is temporarily being interrupted.
- Bear in mind that this does not mean that you no longer see the need to carry out the programme.
- Remember that in time you can simply start the programme again.

Consider the following:
The appraisal gives you the opportunity to make a link to the next time the inappropriate behaviour occurs. This gives the child clarity. It underlines your place as the adult in the hierarchy, and shows the child that you have an active work attitude, and *are ready* to deal with this, regardless of whether or not the child's behaviour is inappropriate. Consistently identifying the next practice situation anchors the child in the growth model. As a result of your attitude, you make a more energetic impression. You no longer have to waste energy hoping that the inappropriate behaviour will not recur. That can only lead to new disappointments and feelings of powerlessness, which in turn signal to the child that you *are not ready* to deal with this.

In the post-active phase you discuss the child's efforts to get a grip on his behaviour. You do this with the help of growth-promoting, non-threatening language. But you also tell the child in a neutral tone that you will continue to practice in this manner. That means that the child can expect you to apply exactly the same sanction whenever the inappropriate behaviour occurs. That is why in the context of the programme, every post-active moment is also a pro-active moment. "Say what you mean."

The appraisal may uncover flaws which did not crop up until this round of the programme. The post-active moment – the appraisal – can provide an opportunity to reach a more precise agreement with the child. The appraisal of the intervention can help to fine-tune strategies. For example, a difficult situation may have arisen when the sanction was applied. The child may have been aggressive, the adults outnumbered, or there was some other reason why the sanction failed. In that case, you can announce new programme elements during the post-active part of the programme, which then automatically become a pro-active step.

Why is it so important to maintain focus? Because repetition is the key. During the appraisal you make it clear to the child that the programme is not finished yet. As soon as the inappropriate behaviour recurs, the child is given the announced warning and if necessary the relevant sanction. But your repetition must be consistent. It is important that you do not weaken your efforts to apply the programme. Keep in mind that ignoring inappropriate behaviour "just this once", for example because "the child has to eat" or "the child has to sleep" or "be on time for school" or "otherwise he will take it out on his brother" is already a sign of losing focus. We call this a content leak, and it is explained on page 115, Appendix C.

The content leak consists of finding excuses based on content for not carrying out the announced educational measure. What this amounts to is **not meaning what you say**. In terms of the programme, you have been consistent only up to step five. Your leverage disappears and the child feels no pressure to develop other behaviour. The content leak can also occur without a programme, in any situation that requires an educational decision. That would be a case of **not saying what you don't mean**. The child is adept at identifying this as your Achilles' heel. If he can exploit this by getting you to lose focus, the child can take control of the educational situation again. Your threats are no longer a worry to him. However, you may be unaware that this loss of focus is what reinforces the child's inappropriate behaviour. This is often the primary reason to start on a programme such as this.

Loss of focus may be temporary, something that happens when it just isn't your day. Even though the programme is progressing well, you may find yourself becoming angry again, shouting, or allowing too much inappropriate behaviour to take place. If so, stop yourself at any point, be clear, and restart the programme immediately. Say something like: "Oh, now I'm doing it again myself! That's not what we agreed. I'm sorry. From now on we'll carry on as planned." You can expect the child to want to hold on to his newly acquired control. "Listen, if you're not doing it, neither am I!" You can give a simple answer: "Yes, you're right, this was wrong. But now we are starting over and you know what you can expect." This should not be followed by a talk or discussion. If the child repeats the behaviour you were practicing on, the agreed procedure should start immediately. The child will probably indicate that this is very unfair, and that you cannot expect him to participate. However, you have recovered and are not willing to discuss it.

This chapter described practical aspects of the post-active intervention, the last of the three sub-interventions. The combination of the sub-interventions is consistently applied to the inappropriate behaviour you are working on. It may be necessary to do this many times before the behaviour improves. A new situation will arise during or after the intervention. This situation can be mapped out with the help of the first step of this programme. Once you have successfully practiced on a number of behaviours, you may notice that the child's general behaviour has improved. This can happen even if you have not worked through all of the points on your original list. You can stop this programme if the child's functioning level shows sufficient improvement with respect to the different problems you were training. You can resume the programme at any time to deal with chronic or recurring problems. Continue to practice, always seeing the programmes as an opportunity to deal with significant behavioural problems.

This book can be used as a manual, as well as a reference book for technical questions about dealing with behavioural problems. If you have motivational problems it may be helpful to go through the first steps again as described in chapters 1 and 2. The book describes the manner in which interventions can be applied to children with significant behavioural problems. Such children function at a lower level in one or more areas. It takes practice for you, the adult, to be able to carry out this programme with success.

If you have carried out the programme properly, and the child still shows little or no improvement, it is advisable to consult a child psychiatrist, even if the child has already had previous psychiatric treatment. The fact the programme has been carried without success may have diagnostic value.

Appendices

Appendices

A. The intervention   99

B. The sanction   105

C. The Metaphors
1. The orchard metaphor   111
2. Taking your autistic child to a street party   112
3. The football metaphor   112
4. Fences in the mud   113
5. Growth-promoting language   113
6. Content-related leak   115
7. The you-bin   116

D. The Portraits

Portraits of a younger child
1. The draw of the passive work attitude   117
2. The empty threat   118
3. Recovering from a lapse   120
4. Taking back control of the classroom   121
5. Proper use of the programme   122

Portraits of an older child
1. An educational vacuum   124
2. Losing control again   124
3. The cautious vice principal   126
4. The partial intervention in a complex situation   127
5. When no programme works   129

E. The Quick Reference Section   131

What is this chapter about?

The six chapters of this manual refer to concepts and metaphors which are explained in further detail in these appendices. In this way you do not have to interrupt the instruction process, but can always refer to an appendix for an explanation. The appendices also contain ten extensive portraits of younger and older children with serious behavioural problems.

A. The intervention

* Intervention is interaction: methodology

This manual was designed to be used on the shop floor. It is however based on the following concept.

Before starting the intervention you have mapped out the situation and repaired your own work attitude. The intervention, which takes place on the "shop floor", is the part of programme that involves the child. This means that there will be *interaction with the child* during the intervention. Just reading about a particular problem – the WHAT – will not build the experience you need to tackle a problem. During the interaction with the child we are primarily concerned with HOW to approach the problem. How do you respond when a child says: "Take your stupid stickers and get lost!" or if he knows just how to locate your Achilles' heel? Or if the inappropriate behaviour continues even though the child has agreed to stop?

The behavioural sciences customarily work with the biopsychosocial model. This is an organisational model that regards behaviour as the outcome of an interaction between biological, psychological and social factors. It makes it possible to evaluate various factors in a neutral manner. A particular scientific explanation of a situation may apply until new research results are available. It is a general model that provides insight into the complexity of this WHAT.

This type of thinking has many advantages. In the medical sciences it has led to evidence-based medicine, and treatment based on national or international guidelines. However, a criticism of this methodology is that it leads to reductionist views of complex diagnostic or treatment situations. Actions that have to be carried out in complex and changing real-life situations cannot be described purely in content-based terms.

The key concept is the difference between WHAT and HOW. WHAT is concerned with content and causality. HOW is concerned with the method. We require a methodological theory of organisation in addition to a content-based theory of organisation such as the biopsychosocial model. The situation on the shop floor is always complex and subject to change. That is why this content cannot be standardised. But your method of working can. A number of methodological domains were used for the workshops that preceded this manual, and for the manual itself. They are described here briefly in lay terms, as opposed to scientific terms.

Process thinking
Process thinking involves thinking about the steps that can be taken, and their sequence and timing. It can reveal hitches in the process. These hitches may occur before or after the moment when the process falters. You can influence the moment at which the process falters by undertaking actions before or after that point. This is something that can be controlled.

An example is the advice given to schools about behavioural problems. We were able to reduce classroom behavioural problems by dividing the school day into parts. Then we identified the moment during a child's day when a problem arose, and subsequently showed up in the classroom. Interventions were moved from the reactive management of escalations to the pro-active management of preliminary stages in places other than the classroom. Including both the pro-active and the post-active moments in the intervention takes the pressure off the reactive moment. This book uses the moments before and after the point at which the process falters to help both the child and the adults learn how to manage behavioural escalations.

System thinking

No child lives alone. A child has a home environment, a school environment and a leisure environment. That is why an intervention on the shop floor can never be aimed solely at the child. This makes matters more complex, and explains why a methodology is required. The methodology should focus not only on the child's problem but also on his interaction with his environment. System thinking does not refer to the aforementioned content-based biopsychosocial systemic model, but to a methodology: a systemic manner of working. An example can help to explain this. You might say: "A child with a problem will do better if his teacher is not stressed." This is logical, and if the teacher is stressed, a child with a problem will behave even worse. But the intervention will be aimed at the child, even though you would like to conduct an intervention on the teacher, or the school. That is why it is important to identify the other parties on the shop floor – for example **children, parents, school, carers** – and not just the child with the behavioural problem. When devising a strategy for dealing with a behavioural problem, you should routinely ask yourself whether an intervention is necessary for one of the other parties. When you intervene in one party's behaviour, you should routinely ask yourself what the consequence will be for the other parties. A child with behavioural problems cannot be isolated from the other parties and the influence they have on one another. The behavioural programme needs to take these reciprocal influences into account, and that is why this manual always refers to interactions.

Functional thinking

Evidence-based medicine is one of the blessings of our times. We have standardised procedures for the treatment of illnesses which require, for example, stomach ulcers to be treated in the same manner everywhere. Guidelines are issued to achieve this and determine the quality requirements that medical staff must satisfy. However, these are the laws that apply in medical consulting rooms. In the behavioural sciences, these guidelines have limited applicability. Uniform treatment is possible only if ailments and problems can be divided up into compartments. Guidelines and other advice often do not cover the entirety of the complex reality of the shop floor. And the shop floor is where parents, teachers, and social workers are in daily contact with the children's behavioural problems. They are not familiar with the guidelines, and would probably not find them helpful if they were. In some cases, giving inappropriate behaviour a name such as OCD, CD or ADHD can even have an adverse effect. It suggests that behaviour is determined by the label it is given, and that labelling will tell us what needs to be done when an incident occurs. In the workshops that preceded this manual, the term *disorder* was replaced by the concept of *level of functioning*. We explained that a child's level of functioning is affected by many more factors than just the disorder. This concept also reflects the fact that the child is embedded in three different environments. The level of functioning can vary each day, for each child, for each of the child's areas of functioning, and each situation. You may not always know why, but you will notice when the child is functioning at a lower, or sometimes even at a higher level. Even if the child has a disorder, the level of functioning may vary, just as a child with diabetes may experience hypoglycaemia, but not every day.

It also became apparent that most parents and teachers were able to draw a rough distinction between these three levels of functioning: high, intermediate and low. They were therefore able to learn how to work with a child functioning at one of the three levels. They saw, for example, that it is possible to talk to and reach agreements with children functioning at a high level. Less talking works better for children functioning at the intermediate level, where some type of reward programme can be used to develop better behaviour. If the level of functioning is low, scaling back inappropriate behaviour is the best approach. Things improved significantly when workshop participants stopped trying to have "a good talk" with children who function at a low level. They discovered why reward programmes were unsuccessful and learned not to expect too much from a child functioning at a low level. And why it is important to address the child at his actual level of functioning. The instructions in this book are all based on the child's actual level of functioning.

This programme is geared to children whose behaviour is inappropriate, and who function at a low level. If one aspect of a child's behaviour functions at the intermediate level, you can work on developing bits of good behaviour. Sometimes a combination of scaling back bad behaviour and building good behaviour is possible. If the child is functioning at a high level, a behavioural intervention is often unnecessary.

Three methodological principals are integrated into this behavioural programme, and this is reflected in the emphasis on the following:
* form   →   growth-promoting language
* process   →   timing
* content   →   level of functioning
In this programme all interventions are based on this methodological structure.

* Intervention is interaction: practical situations

This section moves from methodological explanations to a number of practical examples of the interactional situations you may encounter when applying the intervention on the shop floor.

Destabilisation of the adult
A child confronted with a behavioural programme may try to get out of it. You, as the adult, can expect the child to make various attempts – some of them very determined – to change your mind. He tries to destabilise you, make you feel uncertain about your new strategy, for example by telling you that what you are doing is "infantile". This is a direct personal attack on the weaknesses in your skills as a parent, teacher or childcare worker. It is as if the child is saying "How lame it is to have to get help from someone else. That just proves how incompetent you are!" If you enter into this argument, you are taking part in a battle being played out on the child's favourite territory. So far, this battle has not produced any steps in the right direction. It has in fact firmly guided you in the direction of a passive work attitude and familiar black-and-white patterns. This is a good time to remind yourself that you have started a training programme, and the child will try to get out of it. Simply say: "Yes, I think it's infantile too, and I hope it won't be necessary for too long."

Outsmarting you
Another form of non-cooperation is trying to outsmart you. Both younger and older children use this tactic. The child may appear to be even more dogmatic than you are, and when you try to start the behavioural training, the child attempts to change the programme, improve, discuss, undermine or even expand it.
At first glance, this may seem cooperative, but the child is in fact trying to stay in control, and therefore to avoid taking part in the behavioural programme. It may take the adult some time to recognise this behaviour. Your response should be straightforward. You identify the continual attempts to outsmart you as new inappropriate behaviour and announce a sanction for it. It usually works well to give the child some latitude

by saying: "You can spout all your good ideas for another five minutes but then I'll raise my hand and if you are not quiet within fifteen seconds, a sanction will follow." This five-minute investment can help you avoid a great deal of frustration. The child understands that he has five minutes leeway, and that you are still the one in charge.

Practicing individual aspects of behaviour
In this phase of the programme you choose one aspect of the inappropriate behaviour to practice on. Remember the football metaphor on page 112 of Appendix C. You work on one small aspect because tackling the whole problem is not feasible. Practicing on one small aspect of the inappropriate behaviour helps you, the adult, to train your own work attitude, which is a difficult task in itself. It is above all your own work attitude that will determine the success of the child's training programme.

Where the warning is given
Young children naturally receive different sanctions than older children. Nevertheless, the lead-up and the need for consistency are the same. Use the warning in the reactive moment, and tell the younger child in advance that you plan to use it. The child is given a warning when the inappropriate behaviour you are working on occurs. If the child repeats the same behaviour within a given time period, or refuses to stop, the sanction follows. Prepare your warning sign in advance. It could be a yellow card, a gesture, a sound, or a sentence. You and the child can decide together on the sign that the child finds the least obtrusive. You may, for example, want to discuss how the child wants to be warned during a birthday party to avoid loss of face.

Refusing to listen
Sometimes children simply refuse to listen to an adult at all, even during a well-prepared, friendly work session. You do not have to let this throw you off balance. Simply say: "It's a pity you don't want to listen, but tomorrow you'll see that things are going to be different." Or you could say: "I will see if we can talk about this some other time." This makes for a very short work session. The interventions are applied anyway, and the child gradually realises that things have changed. During the post-active moment you will usually have the opportunity to come back to this. You can then address the child in growth-promoting language as if you had started the training programme together.

Additional inappropriate behaviour
Situations may arise in the course of the behavioural programme, which are extremely frustrating or dangerous, but which are not being practiced at that moment. For example, a sanction that takes away television privileges may make the child so frustrated that he starts to shout, or do something even more disruptive. As the adult you now need to take a quick decision based on an active work attitude. You immediately indentify the child's reaction as inappropriate behaviour and give him a minute to stop the behaviour. If the inappropriate behaviour continues after that minute, a sanction in the form of a time out will follow. The child is immediately sent to his room. Again, the length of the time out is not that important. What is important is that the child understands what will happen if he behaves disruptively. When the child has finished the extra time out in his room, the ban on watching television remains in force.

It's just not your day
If the behavioural programme has been underway for some time you may experience an off day. Or even an off week, when you notice that you have a tendency to become angry or argue or become impatient. The spectre of a passive work attitude looms, along with the tendency to see things as black-and-white. Do not be too hard on yourself. These things happen, and you are only human.

If you find yourself responding in black-and-white terms during an incident, you need to stop what you are doing and start again. Stop right in the middle of the argument and say: "Now I'm doing what we had agreed I wouldn't do. I'm sorry, that wasn't my intention. From now on I am going to do what we agreed. That means that the programme will start again in five minutes." When the five minutes are up, give the child the agreed warning sign for inappropriate behaviour, and if the behaviour does not stop, the sanction will follow. You may notice that the child is somewhat disconcerted. Or the child may try to hold on to the ground he has gained by saying: "If you don't do it, I don't have to either!" Don't argue with the child, simply say: "Yes, things went wrong, but now we are starting over again." After the next sanction the child will understand how things now stand.

The behaviour of other children
It is important to understand that the intervention always takes place within a given context, i.e. the child's environment. Other children in the family, classroom or group are always indirectly involved in the training programme for the child with the inappropriate behaviour. In families, a sister or brother may also develop inappropriate behaviour that fills the vacuum left by the child who is being trained. They sometimes do this because they think they will be rewarded with attention. The parents' positive approach to the child with behavioural problems may also encourage a brother or sister to show an interest in a training programme. In classroom situations, other children may object to what they see as the privileged position of the child with the behavioural problem. They have to work and he gets to stand in the hall doing nothing! Teachers do well to avoid discussing the reasons for sending a child to the hall, because of the danger of being goaded into rejecting the child or making ironic or sarcastic remarks to classmates. Keep in mind that you are the trainer and that every child has to train a different type of behaviour.

Work session between two adults
The description of this training programme contains few references to the sometimes complicated interactions between the adults in the child's environment. The adult is almost always addressed in the singular. This places the emphasis on the communication technique and on the interaction between the child and the adult. However, it goes without saying that in a two-parent family, the partners need to be involved and to consult one another to ensure that they are working on the same aspect of behaviour. It is a good idea to set aside five minutes at the end of each day to discuss the programme's progress. Even if things are going well!

Single parents
Sometimes one of the parents is unable or unwilling to participate. This can happen in a two-parent family, or as a result of divorce or single parenthood. This may be disappointing, but instead of dwelling on it, the parent who is carrying out the programme should concentrate on repairing his or her own work attitude so that the behavioural programme can get started. Using your own active work attitude as a starting point, you can explain the training programme to the other parent, who may in time become more interested.

Single parents may want to seek the support of a family member or friend who knows the child well. This third party can be present during certain practice situations, and be authorised by you to help carry out the programme. The child should be clearly informed of this in advance.

Dealing with the family
Training a child with inappropriate behaviour take places within the nuclear family, but sooner or later the extended family will be confronted with the programme. Among them you can expect to find supporters as well as opponents. Do not expect everyone to be understanding. The energy expended on this frustration is better spent elsewhere. Be prepared for the comments, but stay in your role as trainer and do not let yourself be upset by attempts to undermine the programme, which may or may not be intentional. Family members may refuse to discuss these attempts to undermine, or they may simply continue them. In that case you announce that you will have to stay away from family gatherings for a time. Do not expect this decision to meet with immediate approval.

School and parents
This behavioural programme can be used in a school situation, ideally, in combination with the parents. The system used to train behaviour at school is the same as in the home. Regular work sessions are recommended. Cooperation between the school and the parents is not always ideal. If the parents do not acknowledge the problem, or are unable to participate, the school's contact person must be very clear about the necessity and details of the programme. It is important for the school to carry out the programme regardless of parental cooperation. This creates boundaries for the child in the school environment, which make the burden placed on other children and staff more acceptable. The objective is to ensure that the child gets more benefit from school. If a school has to build a kind of intensive care unit around a child to keep him there, that school has reached the limits of its own capabilities. The steps it has taken should be carefully documented so that the situation is clear to parents, and if necessary, to school inspectors. From that point on, a new strategy is required.

Parents and school policy
A less than ideal level of cooperation between parents and school may also take the form of the school's refusal or inability to discuss or participate in a programme. Not all schools are equally well-equipped to deal with behavioural problems at the policy level or on the shop floor. If the school has no policy in this area, the individual talents and skills of teachers may determine whether or not a child can remain at the school. This can take a heavy toll on teachers, as children with behavioural problems often succeed in driving a wedge between the shop floor and the school's policy makers.

Some schools have a policy on behavioural problems, but provide no support or training on the shop floor. In such cases everything depends on the personality, background and experience of teachers. Sometimes there is a policy in place that individual teachers are unable to implement. The child's behavioural problem then becomes a kind of litmus test for the school's organisational problems. In all of these cases, parents feel a lack of support.

B. The sanction

When inappropriate behaviour occurs, you feel it pushing you beyond your limits. The result is frustration and anger. You hope that it will not happen again. Or you do your best to talk to the child about how disruptive the behaviour is. Sometimes you think you have struck a bargain with the child, so when the behaviour resurfaces, you are shocked and very angry. Apparently there was no bargain. A sanction is required. You are leaning towards retribution. It is time for the child to suffer the consequences, and you think that severe punishment is the answer to the inappropriate behaviour.

Unfortunately, children with serious behavioural problems are usually immune to this type of punishment. They learn little from it, and this leads to even more severe, or longer punishments, which are just as ineffective. A child with serious behavioural problems can even goad a parent into hitting him. But he learns nothing from this. A further ban on riding his bicycle for another three weeks? After a few days he has more or less forgotten why he was being punished. The only thing the child remembers is what an unpleasant parent you are. He is not even allowed to ride his new bicycle! Apparently, children functioning at a low level are incapable of learning from punishment that was intended to teach them a lesson. You are talking over their heads.

Every sanction should be part of an intervention. This means that you have thought about it and made the sanction part of a programme. You have designed a strategy especially for the child with a serious behavioural problem, and you are executing it with care. A sanction that is not part of a programme is carried out on an ad hoc basis, and is usually a poorly prepared response to the inappropriate behaviour you hoped would not recur. It is often a response driven by shock and anger. It is a reflection of how the child's behaviour affects his environment, but it is not an effective way of dealing with inappropriate behaviour.

The sanction technique cannot rely on reminding the child of the norms that apply. You also realise that a "good talk" or some type of reward programme also fail to motivate the child to improve his behaviour. You will have to start from the child's actual level of functioning, not the desired level, or the age-appropriate level. The actual functioning level is usually low.

During the workshops that preceded this book, we concluded that severe content-based punishment does not work on children who function at a low level. The sanction proved to be more effective if it incorporated growth-promoting language and good timing. Read about growth-promoting language on page 113, Appendix C, and about timing (process thinking) on page 99, Appendix A.

Timing is a question of stressing the sequence instead of the content of the sanction. An example from the world of dog training can be used to illustrate this. Hitting a dog for inappropriate behaviour results in a frightened dog. If you hit him a half an hour after the crime, the dog does not understand why he is being punished. The dog simply assumes he has a strange, unpredictable boss. If you do nothing, the dog will assume that he is the boss. In general, dogs learn best from a combination of a light swat on the nose when they are bad, and a treat when they are good. This well-known form of behavioural therapy is referred to as shaping. Small sanctions or rewards that are applied immediately are the most effective. If they are repeated consistently, the dog soon learns who is the boss and what you expect from him.

Shaping is a mild technique that can also be used for children. The difference between training children and dogs is that with children you can make good use of the moments before and after the inappropriate behaviour. You can *pro-actively* announce how you intend to *react*: say what you mean and mean what you say. In the reactive moment, everyone involved knows exactly what is going to happen, and in the post-active moment you can discuss how things went.

The sanction in the *reactive moment* is now embedded and can be reinforced in two different ways:
- The *pro-active moment* gives you the opportunity to approach the child when he is functioning at a higher level than during the incident. Using growth-promoting language shows respect for the child, but at the same time makes it clear what the child can expect if the inappropriate behaviour occurs.
- The *post-active moment* gives you the opportunity to use the behavioural programme as a training programme, and gradually to help the child reflect on his behaviour.

Regardless of how low the level of functioning, this programme nudges the child into a model that encourages growth. That is a new experience for a child who has become accustomed to rejection and punishment. No matter how hard the child tries to avoid it he has to face you, the adult, because you are consistently doing what you said you would do, i.e. imposing a mild sanction. You have taken charge again, and in many out-of-control educational situations, this is a novelty for the child. There is no need to worry if the child announces that the punishment is "no big deal". An older child may shrug it off with a "whatever". The effectiveness of the sanction depends on its consistent application, not on its severity.

You use growth-promoting language at both the *pro-active* and *post-active moment*s. In the *reactive* moment all you have to do is what you said you would do, and do so in a friendly manner. This ensures that the sanction is not an angry, unprepared reaction to the child having overstepped the boundaries again.

The following sanctions are mentioned most frequently in this manual.

The time out
The time out is the basis of the sanctions mentioned in this manual. It involves a temporary removal from a group or an activity. Here, this well-known behavioural sanction is embedded between the pro-active and the post-active parts of the intervention. Do not make time outs too long. A period of between five minutes and half an hour is sufficient. For a child functioning at this level, it is not the time spent thinking in the hall that is a learning experience; it is the consistent link between the inappropriate behaviour and a sanction.
The objective is to teach the child how to function in certain situations without showing inappropriate behaviour. A time out can be used when a warning has not had the desired effect; it is usually applied immediately. For example, when a younger child is disruptive during a meal, he can be sent to the hall for five minutes or told to eat in the kitchen for five minutes. When the child returns to the table, his reaction to the intervention should be discussed very briefly in growth-promoting language. If the child behaves inappropriately again, give the warning signal and if necessary apply the sanction. It may be necessary to calmly send the child away from table several times during a meal.

The deferred time out
A time out can be deferred. If for example an older child behaves inappropriately at the table during a training programme, the sanction might consist of not allowing the child to watch a favourite television show later

that evening. It can even work to ban the child from watching the first or second half of the television programme. This helps the child to remember the link between the relevant behaviour and the sanction. A time out for older children can be deferred for even longer. If the inappropriate behaviour occurs on Monday the sanction can easily be deferred until the end of the week, for example, by not allowing the child to go out for the evening, withholding a portion of his pocket money or cancelling a planned weekend activity.

The reverse time out
Physical time outs are not suitable for older children. It is difficult to tuck a teenager under your arm and place him in the hall. The reverse time out can be used in such situations. Imagine you are a single mother with two teenage sons who are acting up at the table. You announce that you are going to leave the table, and if the behaviour continues you calmly pick up your plate and go into your bedroom to eat. This is also a form of temporarily denying children company. The sons will probably try to destabilise you by telling you to "Do whatever you want..." but your calm attitude and consistent action will reduce the number of necessary interventions. Your sons will want you to return to the table.

The reverse time out and serious behavioural problems
A child who has severe temper tantrums often functions at a very low level. This creates difficult and sometimes threatening situations. These children often already have a history of psychiatric treatment. How can this be turned into a project? The child is not capable of reflecting on the tantrums, and may even explode into a rage during a pro-active work session. As the adult you will want to create a safe environment for the child. At the same time you will also be reluctant to allow yourself to be cursed and shouted at. The child needs to have boundaries. In such cases the intervention should proceed as follows. When the child suddenly becomes enraged you give a short, clear explanation of what you are going to do. You are going to apply a reverse time out by withdrawing to another part of the house for a specified period of time, for example, ten minutes. If the child follows you, act as if the child is not in the room. If necessary, go into the bathroom the next time. You announce that you will return in ten minutes time to see how things are. During these ten-minute periods you do not respond to the child. In the post-active phase you can tell the child that you did not respond because you did not want to provoke him. You announce that you will do the same thing the next time.

The child sees that the you, the adult, remain calm during the tantrum, and that you say what you intend to do every time. And because you follow through, you become predictable in times of great distress for the child. In time the tantrums acquire a framework, and where there is a framework, there is scope for discussion. Indirectly, this also gives the adult the chance to take some control over the situation, even if the circumstances are difficult. You can set up an "if-then" programme within a safe context: "if" the child has a temper tantrum, "then" you announce that you are leaving the room for ten minutes. This gives you the opportunity to do a post-active intervention after the tantrum and your reaction to it. For example, you could say that calming down so quickly after you left is a sign of progress. Or that it was "still" difficult for him to calm down during the first round. The *post-active* part of the intervention emphasises the training aspect of the programme.

You are now doing all that you can as the adult. You are highly attuned to the current low level at which the child functions. If you do that well, it soon becomes clear what is needed. Sometimes the child requires such an intense level of involvement that you need to ask yourself whether this is feasible for you. And whether it is feasible in this particular place. Can this be accomplished at home or at this school? If it becomes clear that the intensity of the behavioural problem is too much for you, the family or the classroom, you will need to decide on a different approach. That is true even if the current approach is working "reasonably well". Often, referral to a professional treatment setting is necessary.

The child may gradually gain more control over his behaviour from this point on. Within this safe, positive model he may develop some interest in the training programme. But it is also possible that the child is incapable of benefiting from the leverage that training creates. Not even if you carry out your part of bargain perfectly. Or you may carry out the interventions in the proper manner but find that it is too exhausting to keep this up for a longer period. That is regrettable, but it does clearly show you and any professionals involved that keeping the child at home or in a particular school is not feasible.

The punch card (followed by a time out)
This sanction can be used for older children. It enables you to take charge again in a very difficult educational situation. You set limits on the amount of inappropriate behaviour you are willing to tolerate in the family, the classroom, or in a leisure setting. This may be necessary if an older child simply goes his own way. For example, regardless of any advice, arguments, or bans, the child continues to stay out late just before final exams. He eats and sleeps when he wants to, and does virtually no homework. You can announce a new approach during a work session. You start by showing respect for the child's need for autonomy, and by saying that you no longer want to treat the child like a baby. This is growth-promoting language.

It is very important to give a brief reason in such cases: you can clearly state that you want to treat the child differently, and that you are doing this because you heartily disagree with the child's attitude towards, for example, final exams. You briefly and clearly state what it is you consider inappropriate, and then you announce the sanction. The sanction consists of introducing a punch card. Over the next few weeks – the time remaining until final exams – you will indicate when the child has done something you consider inappropriate, such as staying out too late or going out twice in one weekend. You will not prevent it, but you will punch the card. You have told the child in advance how many punches the card has. The number depends on the time remaining until final exams. If the punch card is full, and the inappropriate behaviour continues, a time out will follow. Like a football player who consistently refuses to play by the rules of the game, the child will now be temporarily banned from play. The child will be subject to a "bed-bath-meal" regimen for a specified period of time. You assume that the child is not interested in the family's activities. If the child comes home too late, the door will be locked. You lock up the house when you want to go to bed. If the child is late for dinner, you assume he has made his own arrangements. Your in-house restaurant is closed but the child will be welcomed back if he observes the rules.

These measures may seem harsh and somewhat cold. However, they mirror the child's behaviour and indicate that the child is being taken seriously. The child is given respect but your response to the inappropriate behaviour is consistent every time. The situation does not have to escalate. Often the child will come around before the punch card is full, but not always. In the latter case the child will have overstepped your boundaries to such an extent that it is probably no longer feasible for him to remain in that setting and, for example, to prepare for final exams at home. If the punch card is full and the child's behaviour escalates into severely disruptive situations at home or elsewhere, it is usually time to call the police. This can also be announced in advance and carried out with consistence.

The content box
This is not actually a sanction. The content box reflects interaction with the child in the educational situation. The playpen provides an obvious analogy: toddlers often do well in a playpen because it gives them a well-defined play area where they can do whatever they want. The area is limited by the playpen's bars. Those boundaries give you the parent the opportunity to do something else without having the room turned upside down.

The relationship between play areas and boundaries also plays a role in the educational situation. In the family, the classroom, or a group, it is best for all parties concerned if the child knows in advance what his play area, or latitude, is. And what will happen if he climbs over the railing.

Every year, just before the child's birthday, the parents can explain to the child how much latitude he has in terms of bed times, how often and how late he can stay out, rules about smoking and drinking, and sleeping over with friends. You can be very clear about what the child can expect if those boundaries are not respected. The child is given more privileges every year, but they are not privileges without boundaries. Being clear about this in advance, and discussing it on a regular basis, lets the child know exactly where he stands in the family or in your classroom or group. It does not matter whether your views on education are more progressive or conservative than those of other adults. What matters is that the child knows where he stands in your family, classroom or group.

It is a question of finding the optimum combination of latitude and boundaries. Giving children too much latitude encourages them to become the kind of person who does not play by the rules. Focusing solely on the boundaries encourages the child to become someone who does no more than carry out orders. Or who ignores the regime altogether and becomes a kind of autonomous radical. As children get older they feel a growing need for autonomy. They want to make their own rules, and if there are serious behavioural problems, parents and educators face a dilemma. The child experiences the boundaries you set as a threat to his autonomy. But if you set no boundaries, the inappropriate behaviour will continue unabated.

The process box described below was developed to deal with the behavioural problems of older children. The content box is the basis of the process box. The difference is that the latitude in the process box consists of time. The latitude is reflected in respect for the older child's desire to think and act autonomously. The boundaries are reflected in the fact that you keep coming back to the issues.

The time out as process box
The time out in the form a process box can be used for older children. It is usually introduced for older children who have a pronounced need for autonomy and more serious behavioural problems. These may vary from failing to study for an approaching exam, sleeping through alarm clocks and arriving at school too late to becoming unapproachable as a result of drug or alcohol use. You unilaterally announce a clearly defined period within which you will not nag the child. During that period you give the child the autonomy he is so anxious to have. The child wants respect for his independence, and he credits himself with having an almost adult level of functioning even though he clearly does not. After the relevant period you hold a neutral work

session. If you have seen no change in the child's behaviour, you ask if he would like your help, or if wants to try it on his own for another defined period. Usually the child chooses another period and makes excuses for why his behaviour has not changed. This may carry on for some time, but at some point you confront the child with the following problem: you are treating him as an adult, the level at which he claims to function, but you have seen no adult behaviour during the specified periods. And exams are just three weeks away.

One of three things can happen now. The first is that the child may suddenly buckle down and start to work. That is a good thing, and you hope it is not too late. The second possibility is that the child breaks down, and announces (usually in tears) that he just can't do it. It may be late in the day, but at least you now have a handle on what needs to be done. The third option is that the child's inappropriate behaviour continues. That is unfortunate but it would have happened even if you had spent all of your time prodding him. Now you calmly announce that you will see if he is able to start over again next year. The offer of help still stands, but you are not losing any sleep over it. The ball is in the child's court, which means that it is clear that if he wants to succeed at this school, he will have to work. If the school or the curriculum is too difficult for him, he will have to seek help.

Extending or shortening the process box
The period during the process box in which you do not have to nag the child can be lengthened or shortened, depending on the situation. In situations that present a danger to the child or to others in his immediate environment, the period should be drastically shortened. Yet even then the decision to grant autonomy, and hence the chance that the child will change his behaviour, remains intact. The advantage is that the inappropriate behaviour is not allowed to continue unchecked for too long.

The extended process box
The period in the process box can be very lengthy, sometimes lasting up to a year or more. This may happen with older children if, in addition to heavy drug use, criminality is also involved. You, the adult, then no longer have any control over the child's inappropriate behaviour. In many such cases the police or the courts will have assumed that control. At that point you may ask yourself whether the process box is still relevant.
The older child does not appear to be capable of playing by the rules at home, in school or in society. Is there any hope? The process box turns out to be a means of maintaining contact in such cases. Those rare moments when you make contact can be regarded as work session moments. You can discuss how difficult it is for the child to get a grip on his behaviour. You can treat the child with respect without colluding with him. You can also tell him that he is always welcome if he wants to try a different approach. Even if nothing comes of it right away, you keep the lines of communication open. The older child will then notice that you are making a distinction between him as a person and his behaviour. These are of course the kind of situations that arise in connection with extremely serious behavioural problems.

Agree to disagree
If you feel you have too little control over the older child's behaviour, it is still important to keep talking to him. You can show respect for his need for autonomy while still calmly discussing the consequences of his behaviour. You can agree to disagree. You may be forced to conclude, for example, that the way things are going the child is not going to pass his final exams. That is not easy to accept, but accepting it is better than breaking off all communication. The child will be confronted with the social consequences of his choices, but he will still be able to backtrack.

C. The Metaphors

1. The orchard metaphor

Imagine you are the owner of an apple orchard. Every autumn the apples ripen. And every autumn boys steal the apples from your trees. This metaphor represents things that happen to you which are unasked for and unwanted. You have two choices. Both of them will make you unhappy. One choice is "white" and one is "black".

"Black" involves a refusal to accept the boys' behaviour. You're not having it! Who do they think they are? You make every effort to prevent a recurrence. You build a big fence around your garden and ask the police to keep an eye on things. You even lie in wait for the boys with a stick in your hand. That will teach them! This costs you a great deal of effort and energy. You have to remain on guard every day. Inevitably, one night you will doze off and the boys will cut a hole in your fence and steal your apples. Despite all your efforts, the apples are gone. You have no control over your garden and you are placed in a passive position. This is unpleasant and very tiring.

"White" involves accepting the boys' behaviour. You leave the gate open so that it does not get damaged. And your apples are stolen. You have no control over your garden and you are placed in a passive position. This is unpleasant, and you feel powerless.

You will appreciate that it is possible to swing back and forth between black and white for a long time. Sometimes black wins. You are furious about what has happened and feel the need to mete out some strict punishment. Sometimes white wins. You resign yourself to your powerless position. You really have no idea what you can do to change all of this. You are in an extremely exhausting, unpleasant situation. Whether you are in the black or the white position, you have no control over the boys' behaviour.

Is change possible? The answer is: yes! You will have noticed that your position in both the black and white situations is described as passive. No matter how much energy you expend, you are in a passive position. However, this metaphor also offers scope for an active position. Put up a sign in the garden that says "Pickers wanted. Reward: a box of apples." The same boys might turn up at your door, who now think "We don't have to steal apples, because if we help pick them we'll get a whole box apples free."

Now something has happened. Regardless of whether or not the plan succeeds, you have taken an active position. You did it by accepting that those boys exist and that it is up to you to do something about their behaviour. Your attitude has changed. Where first you were passive and simply hoping your apples would not be stolen this year, placing a sign in your garden is taking an active position. You make an investment in the form of a box of apples. This is a business risk since there is no guarantee that the plan will work. But the most important change is that you have taken an active position by accepting that the boys exist. You are no longer waiting for events, you have turned this into a project.

This metaphor is about fixing your attitude. It is pointless to start a behavioural programme until your attitude has been fixed. You risk sinking into despair and helpless anger at the recurrence of the inappropriate behaviour, and becoming cynical about any behavioural programme. It also implies that you should not wait around for a golden tip that can solve your child's serious behavioural problems. For example, a one-off piece of advice that worked, or is said to have worked, on another child. Or a simple piece of educational advice that requires little effort on your part but promises to produce quick results.

Arriving at the right behavioural programme takes time and effort. You are learning something. That is why it is important to fix your own attitude before you start to deal with behaviour on the work floor. And remember that in the end failing to do this will require more effort than doing it.

2. Taking your autistic child to a street party

Imagine you are the parents of an autistic child, and you are invited to a street party. You can do two things. You can say : "There we go again. Something fun finally happens in our street and we can't go because we have an autistic child." Or you can say: "If we go, we'll have to agree that one of us will take him home if he starts screaming."

If you choose the second option, the child may start screaming after only five minutes. That is alright. You have tried, and you have a clear agreement. One adult takes him home, the other stays (perhaps to look after the other children) at the street party. "We'll try again next time." If the child does not start screaming, or waits two hours to start, you will have had a fantastic day. "We'll do this more often!"

This is an abbreviated version of the orchard metaphor. They both describe exactly the same thing: fixing your attitude. You assume that the child will start to scream, and if he does, everyone knows what to do next.

3. The football metaphor

Imagine a child who is not very good at football and you want to do something about it. It is important to know what needs to be practiced. You make a list of the football moves he hasn't mastered. You divide them into categories, such as the corner, the pass, the header, and the penalty.

You know that you cannot practice everything at once. You cannot practice headers and penalties at the same time. So you have to choose one category: the penalty. And if you choose that category you know that practicing headers will have to wait. The header technique is not going to improve at this point. So it makes no sense to complain about headers during penalty practice. You know the headers need work, but that is not what you are practicing now. You will come back to them later.

While you are practicing penalties, you divide them into subcategories: placing the ball in the right place, judging the distance, keeping an eye on the keeper's movements, choosing your corner, the run up and kicking technique. Football players have different levels of skills. If you are training an A-team player, you might focus on getting him to aim the ball at the upper left-hand corner. If you are training a beginner you might want to focus on basic kicking techniques.

This metaphor is about setting an agenda for a behavioural programme. The same principle applies; you cannot practice everything at one. You need to make a list of inappropriate behaviours and choose one as a starting point. The list can be divided into categories and even into subcategories. With football it is easier to accept that you cannot train everything at once. In the case of inappropriate behaviour, we tend to feel a greater need to do everything at once. But it does not work here either. We know from experience that starting to practice is the most important aspect of an active approach to behavioural problems. Where you start is not all that important. With younger children, other inappropriate behaviour sometimes improves at the same time. In other words, if you, the adult, take an active attitude and follow this programme consistently, the child's general behaviour may improve, including other inappropriate behaviours on the list. If not, you simply work through the categories one by one.

4. Fences in the mud

If you have the task of cleaning up a large amount of mud, it is difficult to know where to start. The mud is unstructured and you have no clear perspective. You can start by placing fences in the mud. You may not get a clear perspective right away, but you have made compartments. Then you can extract the mud from each compartment and this will gradually produce results. It is all about the technique used to extract the mud. It ensures that you are not overwhelmed by the total amount of mud. That is why it does not matter as much where you begin, as long as you begin.

This metaphor is used as an additional explanation along with the football metaphor. You cannot practice all football techniques at the same time. It illustrates how you do not always have a clear view of all of a child s inappropriate behaviours. Or of any differentiation in or interrelatedness between those behaviours. The solution presented in this metaphor is to start somewhere with just one of the child's inappropriate behaviours. A more differentiated picture will emerge as you go.

5. Growth-promoting language

Behavioural problems can make adults very angry. Your child can often detect an angry, sarcastic or ironic tone in your voice. The child recognises that tone immediately; he has had practice. The anger is your blind spot. It ensures that however well-intentioned you are, you constantly remind the child of the level at which it *should be functioning*. But the child cannot meet this expectation because it functions at a different level. You know from the programme that you have to take control again and be consistent – say what you mean and mean what you say. But this cannot be truly effective until you find the level at which the child actually functions, introduce a coaching model at that level, and speak growth-promoting language.

Growth-promoting language should be used during the pro-active and post-active phases of the intervention. In the reactive phase of the intervention, you only need to do what you said you would do, in a friendly manner.

In the pro-active phase – during your work session with the child – growth-promoting language is used to change the old way of communicating in a language that is full of disappointment and rejection. It is safe to assume that the child is not interested in another round of rejection. He will not listen to your training proposal if you are scolding him at the same time. If he is treated with respect, the child will be surprised, and more inclined to listen. Growth-promoting language gives you the opportunity to show respect, and draw a distinction between the child and his inappropriate behaviour.

Do not say: "It is time for you to listen up, things have got to change." If the child is young, it is more effective to say: "I really think you are too big now to have me following you around like a police officer, telling you what to do." If the child is older, try saying: "Listen Jessica, I've been thinking and you're right, we need to do things differently." Or the slightly more challenging: "I really don't what to treat you like a baby in this respect." Growth-promoting language has to be precise. During the workshops that preceded this manual, a slightly less precise choice of words was often greeted with laughter. "Because you are acting like a baby" is not growth-promoting language. It is just another accusation. The following sentence is also derogatory: "…because I am so tired of having to treat you like a baby…" The child could not care less what makes you tired!

If you tell a teenager that you no longer want to treat him like a child, you are really saying much more. Indirectly, you are telling him that in the recent past you have had to treat him like a child. You had every reason to do that. You are labelling the teenager's behaviour as childish. You are also announcing that you are now going to treat him the way someone his age should be treated, even if he acts childish. He can continue to do so, but now it has consequences. This sentence also tells him that you want to treat him the way someone his age should be treated. You do not begrudge him his autonomy, but you are also challenging him to respect the boundaries. Finally, this technique is also a subtle reminder that you have an overall view of the situation, and are therefore in a position to keep an eye on things.

In the post-active phase, growth-promoting language helps to put a positive label on the child's efforts to control his behaviour. Those efforts are redefined as training. The child is praised for his training efforts. Even if the training was not self-imposed.

Now it is time to use words that emphasise progress or indicate that while it is still hard for the child, you are confident that things will improve. When the child comes back to the table after a time out, things may or may not have gone well out in the hall. If things went well after a 5-minute time out you may be tempted to give the child a compliment: "Well done, come and sit down." But a compliment is not growth-promoting language, because there is no leverage involved. The following greeting does have leverage: "I saw how quickly you calmed down in the hall. You're making progress. You can come back to the table." It is as if you are saying, it was quicker than I expected. You did it yourself. If things did not go so well you say: "I saw that is was still difficult for you to calm down in the hall. Come back to the table." This implies that you expect it to become easier in the future, because of the training.

Language that promotes growth also has to be precise in the post-active phase. A child returns to the group after a successful time-out, and you say: "You see, you can do it!" Or: "Next time, if you think before you start screaming, you can stay at the table…" These are also derogatory remarks. They remind the child that he has not attained the desired level of functioning, not of the effort put into the training project. We put these remarks in the "you-bin". Read more about the you-bin on page 116, Appendix C.

You can see that speaking in growth-promoting language is not pandering to the child. You are not handing out sugar-coated, bitter pills. It is a well-thought out choice of words that focuses on giving the child respect at the level at which it functions. And on suggesting that development is possible. Growth-promoting language does not excuse the child's behaviour; it replaces the expectation of punishment with a growth model. The purpose of speaking in growth-promoting language is to find a way of taking the child seriously while creating a new starting point. The child loses his control over the educational situation, but at the same time he becomes more active because the model encourages development. The adult who uses growth-promoting language is taking charge in a way that is beneficial to the child.

Using growth-promoting language takes practice, especially once you have slipped back into a passive attitude. The essence of the new language is that it motivates both you and the child.

6. Content-related leak

If a child comes into his parent's bedroom at night and says he is afraid, he may be allowed to get into bed with them. The following night he wakes up again and is allowed to sleep in his parents' bed. The father sleeps in the child's bedroom because he has to get up early the next morning. If this carries on, the father will want to return to his bed at some point. However, the mother says: "But the child is so frightened."

There is no agreement as to how the night-time fear should be dealt with. In fact, the mother's comment blocks the father's ability to change the situation. This is a content-related leak: failure to follow through with a necessary or announced educational measure because of a content-related excuse. Content-related leaks occur when there is no programme, in situations that demand an educational decision. It is a case of **not meaning what you haven't said**. The child quickly learns what your Achilles' heel is, and if he continues to seek out those situations in which it occurs, he will inevitably take control of the educational situation. He has nothing to fear from threats.

The content-related leak can also occur while a programme is underway. For example, if you stop doing what you said you would do before the programme has started, it has the effect of a content-related leak. You might give in a little because you think your partner is too strict. You might make up an excuse because you are fed up with the programme. You might think the child just needs a chance to "be himself".

In short, there are all kinds of content-related reasons to deviate from the planned path. This is a case of **not meaning what you say**. In terms of the programme, you have been consistent only up to step five. Your leverage has disappeared, and pressure on the child to change his behaviour has come to an abrupt halt. Remember that the content-related leak occurs when you accept undesirable behaviour "just this once", for example because "the child has to eat" or "the child has to sleep" or "the child has to be on time for school" or "because he'll take it out on his little brother".

The child quickly notices that you are not doing what you said you would do. It is a bit like crying wolf. It works once but the child soon realises there is no wolf. Once again, his position is a comfortable one. And you are in danger of lapsing into a passive attitude. It is important to realise that a content-related leak supports and reinforces undesirable behaviour. It often sparks the need to start a programme such as this.

7. The you-bin

Assume that you are commenting on an action or behaviour. The person you are addressing replies by mentioning something you do not do properly. That is a "you-bin". It indicates that your conversational partner sees your comment as criticism. Criticism they could do without. You do not get a chance to discuss the particular action or behaviour In a constructive manner.

In this programme you want to motivate children functioning at a low level to change their behaviour. It is important to think about the shaping of your interventions. If a time-out results in an improvement in the child's behaviour, it is not helpful to say: "You see, it's much nicer for everyone if you don't scream at the table". Or: "Next time, if you think about it first, we won't have to send you away." These remarks remind the child of the *desired level* of functioning. They remind him that he is a long way from that level. It is important to remember that this programme is about training *at any* level.

If you forget that the child is training at a lower level, the post-active intervention becomes a you-bin for transferring your anger to the child. This does not encourage the development of more appropriate behaviour. Making the child feel as if it has to repeat results already attained places pressure on the child. At this level of functioning, the pressure is demotivating and can cause a relapse of the misbehaviour. After all, you are commenting on the child himself, and not on his efforts to control his behaviour. In other words, you are still rejecting the child.

How can you avoid the you-bin? You can avoid it by concentrating on the child's actual level of functioning, and not on the desired level. You start training at the child's level. You base your comments on that level, and do not expect the child to attain a higher level right away.

D. The portraits

▶ **Younger child**

1. The draw of the passive work attitude

Portrait of a younger child

"He'll never do it!"

The parents of ten-year old Ryan are meeting with a childcare professional to prepare an intervention. The childcare professional has discussed at length the concept of holding a work session at a pro-active moment, as well speaking growth-promoting language and announcing the intervention in advance. When the subject of giving a short time out is raised, the parents exchange glances. "He'll never do it!" says the mother. The parents already know that Ryan will disobey if they give him a time out. They know Ryan. He will become extremely angry if his parents try to take charge and do something about his behaviour. "It will never work. You childcare professionals mean well, but you should spend a day at our house. You would find out soon enough how difficult it is."

The childcare professional notices almost immediately how easily the parents slip back into their powerless position. He also notices that they are no longer listening to him. He cheerfully announces: "It's good that you already know that he will get angry. Now we can be pro-active and incorporate that into the intervention." Speaking to an imaginary Ryan during a work session, the childcare professional says, "Sending you to the hall may make you very angry with us Ryan. But if you misbehave, you can expect to get an extra sanction." The childcare professionals discusses the added sanction with the parents. It should be announced right away, so that Ryan knows where he stands.

The childcare professional can tell from the parents' surprised faces that they are getting interested in the plan again. He explains that children with behavioural problems almost always object to the sanction that has been announced. It is better to assume that the added sanction will be necessary. If you know what to expect, there is no need for disappointment when it happens. Moreover, you know precisely what is going to happen, and so does Ryan.

This portrait shows that parents have to get used to a new approach. They are understandably wary of the programme and of the person explaining it to them. Seeing is believing, and they know just how bad things are in the family, and how many different tactics they have tried on Ryan. The childcare professional had better have a good plan!

We also see how parents can get sucked into a passive work attitude. Here both parents have retreated into the "white" position described by the orchard metaphor on page 111 of Appendix C. The childcare professional does well to avoid a complex discussion of the origins of their passive work attitude. He does not have to confront them with substantive psychological considerations. At best this will lead to an interesting discussion, but it will not help the parents deal with Ryan's behaviour. The question is, what should they do when an intervention makes Ryan so angry?

It is comforting for the parents if the childcare professional assures them that this happens all the time, and that the programme takes it into account. He cheerfully announces that it is a good thing that the parents already know that they can expect complications. This breaks their deadlock. He knows that these parents have made many attempts to deal with Ryan's behaviour. They have had to face many disappointments, and they will be easily discouraged if things go wrong "yet again". It is understandable that they freeze up in such situations and immediately revert to a passive position in the hope of avoiding further disappointment.

The childcare professional offers the possibility of an extra sanction as a simple addition to the programme. He is demonstrating that the principle of the pro-active work attitude comes down to **saying what you mean and meaning what you say***. Beforehand you try to explain as clearly as possible what you consider inappropriate behaviour, and what the child can expect if it occurs. If the parents expect a difficult reaction from Ryan, they can incorporate this into the programme. Ryan will notice that his behaviour and his reaction to the announcement no longer succeed in making his parents feel disappointed and powerless. He sees that they have taken back control of the situation. Ryan may think up new ways to make his parents angry. It is a good idea to realise in advance that these are Ryan's efforts to stay in control. The parents can interpret this as a sign of a lower level of functioning, and cheerfully respond by saying: "Alright, it's a good thing we caught this now, Ryan. Now we can do something about this too."*

If the parents are able to deal with Ryan's frustrating behaviour in this manner, they can immediately extricate themselves from the passive work attitude. They are in the driver's seat and have taken control. They are no longer intimidated by Ryan's reaction because they know what to expect. This is true during the preparation of the intervention, but also when something unexpected happens while it is being carried out. They are prepared for Ryan's unexpected reactions, and see this as a project, not a disappointment. Their attitude no longer radiates powerlessness and disappointment. It is as if they are letting Ryan know he will be held accountable for whatever inappropriate behaviour he displays. And Ryan will gradually find out that his parents mean what they say.

2. The empty threat

Portrait of a younger child
"Saying what you mean and meaning what you say"
Daniel, Max, Caitlin, and their parents are spending the day in an amusement park. Caitlin was allowed to ask a friend to come with her, since there are already two boys. Daniel's father gives him an advance warning: "We are here to enjoy ourselves today, and I will be keeping an eye on you. If I see you teasing Caitlin and Lauren, we will go home immediately." He gives Daniel a meaningful look, to ensure that he understands what he has said. Daniel nods.

Things go well for the better part of the morning. The parents plan a timely break for food and drinks, and after that they decide to ride an old-fashioned carrousel. As the children run towards the ride, Daniel sticks out his foot and trips Caitlin, who gashes her knee. The first aid post bandages the wound and Daniel is given a warning: "You heard what I said, didn't you? You're lucky I didn't take you home." Daniel nods. After lunch Daniel pulls Lauren off the teeter totter, because he wants he sit on it. Lauren slaps Daniel, who becomes so angry he hits her back, very hard. His father threatens: "One more time ..." Daniel calms down and nods. A third incident spoils the parent's mood for the rest of the day. They start complaining about how Daniel always ruins their outings. They drive home in silence.

The parents apparently realise that Daniel is likely to behave inappropriately during a trip to an amusement park, but they do not to take any real precautionary measures. They seem to be hoping that on a special day like this he will agree to a temporary ceasefire. However, that is not possible, given Daniel's low level of functioning. The father in this portrait says what he means, but does not mean what he says. He hopes that threatening to leave will do the trick. A trip to an amusement park is costly, and he does not want the other children to suffer because of Daniel's behaviour. But Daniel is soon wise to his father's empty threats. Not only are the threats ineffective, they actually contribute to the child's bad behaviour. Daniel has nothing to fear because he knows his father will not follow through. In the end the family pays a high price as the situation gets out of hand.

If we examine what Daniel's father does when he gives his warning we see that he believes that Daniel recognises his authority. He thinks that penetrating looks will help to convince Daniel that he had better behave himself. He does not use growth-promoting language. Instead he hopes that the threat of a severe content-based intervention will keep Daniel in line. Even though he is well-intentioned, the threats Daniel's father makes reflect a passive attitude. He chooses the "black" view. However, when it is time for the intervention to take place, he repeats his "black" warning but his actions are "white".

Children with behavioural problems immediately recognise this inconsistency. Daniel now realises that he can do whatever he wants. All he has to do is close his ears when his parents start to preach at him. And he has a lot of experience with that... If his parents choose going home as a sanction, they must hold a work session with Daniel and explain it to him beforehand. Daniel needs to know what he is not allowed to do, and if he misbehaves anyway or refuses to stop after a warning, they actually need to leave immediately.

Alternative sanctions are possible. The father could be more lenient and say: "If I have to give you more than three warnings we will go home. We can visit the amusement park another day." Daniel's father could do this proactively, but also reactively, for instance if he and his wife had forgotten to prepare for the outing. Daniel gets a card with three punches. He should be told in advance precisely what counts as inappropriate behaviour and when he can expect to have the card punched. If the card is full and Daniel behaves inappropriately again, the trip to the amusement should end immediately. That signals that his father says what he means and means what he says.

Another variation consists of giving time outs in the park. One of the adults stays with Daniel in one spot for the agreed length of the sanction while the others continue to enjoy the amusement park. This should be a neutral place that is clearly less fun than the ride he is missing out on, and he should not be allowed to make up for the lost ride. When the sanction is over, Daniel and his parent join the rest of the family. There is no need for the parent who remains with Daniel to act angry. The sanction is the result of the fact that Daniel's level of functioning is too low to participate in the outing. "We'll try again later" is all that the parents need to say. If Daniel requires many time outs they clearly need to have a different plan for the next time, but at least they will not have spoiled the day for the others.

This portrait demonstrates how pro-active planning reduces risk, but also how failing to carry out the sanction you have pro-actively announced can destroy your credibility.

3. Recovering from a lapse

Portrait of a younger child

"When it just isn't your day"

Jack's father and mother have designed a good behavioural programme for him, but it is difficult to remain consistent. For an eleven-year old, Jack's verbal skills are well-developed. His mother sighs that she has to stay alert all day long and be very careful about what she says. She thinks the behavioural programme is a good idea, but she feels as if she never has a moment's rest. Jack's mother has three other children and a busy life. Fortunately her husband is also participating in the programme so she does not have to do everything on her own. Especially now that her father is sick and she often has to drive him to the hospital for radiation treatments.

With her daughter Chloe at home with the measles it is difficult for the mother to do everything properly. It is almost as if Jack was waiting for this moment. He becomes very difficult, whining and showing a lot of the inappropriate behaviour they had been working on. It is all too much for Jack's mother. "Why are you so obnoxious? Can't you behave yourself for just one day?" Jack is now on familiar ground and he is ready to do battle. He says: "You should talk! You've been stomping around barking orders and shouting all day. Don't blame me for that." His mother is drawn into the argument, saying that she has to do everything herself, while Jack, as the oldest child, might have a little consideration for the fact that she is very busy now that both grandfather and Chloe are sick. Jack is quick to reply that his mother makes it hard for herself. She wants to do everything herself, even though Aunt Geraldine could easily take grandfather to the hospital. You enjoy stress!" The mother realises that she needs to walk away or she will start throwing things. She really feels like having a good cry.

Sometimes you are just too busy. Sometimes it is just too hard for the adult to keep all of the balls in the air, but remember that a child with behavioural problems is an expert at finding your Achilles' heel. It does not take much effort on his part to make you angry. Doing so reinstates the old situation. It is a pyrrhic victory for the child and you feel like a beetle on its back waving its legs. Completely powerless.

In this battle, the argument is a dubious weapon. For children with behavioural problems, arguments always degenerate into an "I said-you said" power struggle. You will never win an argument on the basis of content and trying to convince the child of the merits of your point of view. The child is not looking for a reasonable discussion but for an opportunity to take control again. For the child, having a discussion equals not changing the inappropriate behaviour. In the meantime you are desperately trying to find rational arguments that will change that behaviour or enable you to get a grip on the situation.

Some children have very well-developed argumentative skills. They externalise matters and lay the blame somewhere else. If everything is the fault of the stupid teacher, his sister, or the rain, the child has an excuse for not cooperating with any plan. They dominate the discussion and corner you, so that all you can do is react. That is what happened to the mother in this portrait, who quickly became angry and discouraged.

There is an alternative. As the adult you can become more aware of how you end up in a black or white position in the reactive moment. Once you realise this you can quickly recover by saying: "Okay, let's stop right here. What I'm doing is wrong. From now on we'll do it the way we agreed. That means that from now on you will get a sanction if you behave inappropriately." The child says: "Yes, but you were doing it too, so I don't have to stop!" You say: "Yes, that was a mistake, but now the rule is in force again." If the child persists, claiming that he still has at least two more chances, you need to be firm. "We are going to do what we agreed." Any further protests should be regarded as additional inappropriate behaviour. Say for example: "You can complain about this two more times, but on the third time the sanction will come into effect."

The sequence is as follows: you realise that you are slipping into the passive position; you stop the discussions immediately, apologise for interrupting the training session, and re-establish the hierarchy. If the child tries to test whether you mean what you say, a warning will follow. If the behaviour does not stop, the announced sanction will come into effect.

This portrait demonstrates how you, the adult, can deal with your own contribution to the failure of an intervention by turning a reactive moment into a pro-active moment. It is a useful technique for those off days, but it also helps you to become more aware of your own tendency to get caught up in a an argument.

4. Taking back control of the classroom

Portrait of a younger child
"I've had enough of this"
The class is very disruptive. You, the teacher, have called for order several times, but the children are excitable and impertinent. When one boy and his chair tumble over the whole class bursts out laughing and everyone is talking at once. You are irritated and you shout to the class: "I have had enough of this." You add a few choice comments that you immediately regret. But you also think the children should realise how hard your job is, and understand that you have reached the limits of your patience. You announce that the entire class will have to remain seated after the bell. "That will teach them," you conclude grimly. However, you are also angry about your own powerlessness. Why is it so difficult to keep this class under control? What on earth can be done about it?

What on earth can you do? You have tried so many times to reason with unruly children. But your intervention is not based on the actual level at which these children function. They are not open to reason. You are losing your grip, and that makes you angry. You lose your temper and impose a reactive punishment, because you believe that suffering the consequences of their behaviour will teach them a lesson. Your work attitude has become passive, and you are trapped in a black and white situation.

Because you are troubled by your own irritability you discuss the matter with the school's counsellor. She reminds you of the training you received last year, and together you review the methods you learned. When the term "work attitude" crops up you remember something about starting with repairing your own attitude. And about learning to accept that sometimes classrooms are noisy places, and the way to deal with this is to make a project out of it. Both you and the counsellor realise that the school still does not have a consistent policy for dealing with behavioural problems.

Let's assume that you have decided to make a project out of this problem. The first question concerns the nature of the intervention. How do you take back control of an unruly classroom? It helps if the teacher is no longer frustrated. You start by accepting the problem: the class is unruly and is likely to remain so for the rest of the day. It is better to see the classroom situation as a reflection of the children's lower level of functioning than as an interactional problem between you and the children. You can calmly devise a strategy, even while the class is unruly, but you should also not expect to be able to take back control that same day, or afternoon or hour.

This immediately changes your work attitude: you are no longer an adult who has lost his or her place in the hierarchy, but an adult who is not visibly affected by the class's current behaviour. This is not an indifferent or sarcastic work attitude; it is calm and professional. The timing of the intervention helps you to make a reactive situation pro-active. This involves calmly announcing that you no longer want to treat the class like babies (growth-promoting language). You know that it is sometimes difficult for them to be calm (brief reason). You are going to help them in the following way (re-establish the hierarchy and announce the sanction). Tell the class that you will give them a warning sign next time (raising your hand or a yellow card). If the classroom or the child in question does not stop the inappropriate behaviour within a minute the sanction will follow. The children now know what the sanction is and when it will be imposed. That may happen in the next hour, the next part of the day or the following day.

You, the teacher, will have a better grip on the class if you do not become too stressed about the situation that has arisen. You can save time by viewing the situation as a practice situation for the next time. Keep in mind that this strategy is only possible if the situation presents no immediate threat to the other children in the class. If it does, safety is your first concern, and a reactive intervention is required. But such incidents should also lead to clear agreements about what will happen the next time.

5. Proper use of the programme

Portrait of a younger child
"Outsmarting the teacher"
Amanda, the year 7 teacher, is attending an afternoon meeting to discuss problem pupils. She has urgent questions about the behaviour of Lucy, an intelligent 10-year old in her class. Lucy is a nice girl but she can also become very angry, especially when something happens to her that she considers unfair. It may be in response to a reprimand from a teacher or to something that happens on the playground. When Lucy is angry she swears and throws things, and sometimes she even physically attacks another pupil. It is impossible to reason with Lucy when she is in a rage. She shouts and hurls insults. Fortunately these tantrums are short-lived. Afterwards Lucy is always sorry, but everyone is upset. Amanda finds that it does not help to lecture Lucy, and discussions about why she is so angry also lead nowhere. She says it just happens, as if it is happening to someone else.

The behavioural therapist tells Amanda about the programme described in this book. Amanda is advised to talk to Lucy in advance about what will happen if she has another temper tantrum. Amanda welcomes the fact that she will even be able to do something about Lucy's behaviour during the brief run-up to a temper tantrum. Lucy will be given a five-minute time out, which she will spend in an agreed location outside of the classroom. Practicing during the period before a temper tantrum is intended to help Lucy control her own behaviour.

Amanda rushes out of the room immediately after receiving the advice. There has already been an incident with Lucy today and she is waiting in the classroom. Amanda has told her that her behaviour was so disruptive that she would have to discuss it with the other teachers. Ten minutes later Amanda is back in the meeting. She has a question for the behavioural therapist. She has carefully explained everything to Lucy, who thought it was a good plan. "But", said Lucy "can I have a ten-minute time out? At least then I can play on my computer!" What should Amanda do about this?

Lucy is a smart girl. She wants to cooperate with Amanda's plan and she even has a better suggestion. At first glance this might seem like a cooperative attitude. But it is in fact an attempt on Lucy's part to stay in control by outsmarting the teacher (See the explanation on page 101, Appendix A). Amanda is being badgered into considering whether Lucy's proposal is better than her own. It sounds so reasonable: if Lucy stays away ten minutes, she can make good use of her time. What could be wrong with that? Amanda is wavering. She appreciates the fact that Lucy is finally thinking about her own behaviour, but she has a suspicion that she is not entirely in control of this strategy.

What is going on here? When Lucy is having a temper tantrum, there is no reasoning with her. The intervention that Amanda explained to her is intended for just such a moment. Something is wrong here. Lucy is trying – intentionally or unintentionally – to outsmart the teacher. Because she is thinking about the content of the sanction, it seems possible to strike a bargain with her about her behaviour. But the intervention was necessary because Lucy does not keep up her end of a bargain. Lucy's better idea has only one purpose: to stay in control. Amanda needs to take the lead and stay in control in a firm but friendly manner. The plan is meant to protect Lucy from her own anger, and to help her control her own behaviour. Amanda could say that she understands that it is not easy for Lucy, but that for now, this is how things will be done.

There is something else wrong with Lucy's proposals. It makes no sense if the "sanction" Lucy is given just before a temper tantrum is something she actually enjoys, i.e. playing with her computer outside of the classroom. This sanction seems more like a reward, and could even increase the frequency of the temper tantrums. A sanction does not have to be severe, but it should not be so attractive that it encourages the inappropriate behaviour.

During the weeks that follow, Lucy responds fairly quickly to the programme. However, Amanda has her hands full in the classroom and she often forgets to do the post-active intervention. She also forgets to set aside five minutes at the end of the day to talk about how things went. The next day, when Lucy is on the point of getting a time out, Amanda says, "You remember what we agreed, don't you?" Lucy's response is recalcitrant.

In this portrait we see that the teacher forgets not only the post-active intervention, but also the use of growth-promoting language. This may be the result of the pressures of the classroom, or Amanda's inexperience with the programme. She seem to be satisfied with the return of "normal" behaviour, and more interested in the results than in the training aspect of Lucy's programme. This weakens the programme. It is the post-active phase that confirms the training aspect of the programme, and gives the teacher the chance to compliment Lucy's efforts. Identifying it as training helps Lucy when she is functioning at a lower level, because everyone realises that training takes time. But it is also good for Lucy to be challenged to function at a higher level. Functioning at an age-appropriate level is the objective of the programme.

▶ **Older child**

1. An educational vacuum

Portrait of an older child
"What can a mother do?"
Troy has just turned fourteen. He wants to follow in his father's footsteps and start a handyman service, which is why he does not think that many of the things he learns at school are very useful. Like most of the boys in his class, Troy smokes. His father, who has little time (or interest) in spending time with Troy, gives him a packet of cigarettes every week, which he shares with his friends. If he asks his father for another packet, he gives it to him.

His mother is very opposed to Troy's smoking at such an early age. When she explains this to Troy he says he doesn't have to listen to her. Trying to talk to her husband about it just makes him angry, and he tells her to stop nagging. The mother is not ready to give up and she says: "He's my child! I don't have to stand by and let my husband keep him supplied with cigarettes!" The father promises to stop but the next day he gives Troy a packet of cigarettes. His mother sighs: "What can a mother do?"

Troy's father has little involvement in his son's upbringing, although he lectures him every now and then. His wife takes care of everything in the family, and this suits everyone as long as there is no trouble. But when problems arise, Troy's mother cannot manage on her own. And his father is not used to getting involved.

Any educational issues surrounding Troy create an immediate vacuum. The mother, who is used to taking care of everything herself, is sidelined. Her husband exacerbates the problem by not taking a stance. Troy naturally takes his father's side. Both parents want the best for their son but they have never discussed his education or how to deal with incidents such as this. Both seem satisfied when all is well. The mother can do things her own way, and she usually finds that this is the quickest solution. The father is not bothered by the children, and that suits him just fine. He works hard just to put food on the table.

However, if you object to smoking, especially at such a young age, you have an educational problem that needs to be solved. And it is usually an unsolved problem that leads to the kind of trouble that these parents do not like.

This portrait shows how adults can get caught up in their emotions, both by ignoring problems as well as by trying to do everything alone. Neither attitude provides an adequate solution for the educational problem. It is good to be aware of this as it can contribute to inappropriate behaviour.

2. Losing control again

Portrait of an older child
"Provoking your brother"
Adam is a year younger than his brother William. William is a difficult child, and his parents have frequently consulted therapists about his behaviour. Over the years he has had a lot of extra attention from his parents, who have done their best not to let his problems affect the others in the family. They have made a point of doing

things with Adam and his younger sister Charlotte as well. Lately, William's behaviour has improved, and his parents feel they can finally take a breather after all their efforts. For once they were even able to see a film together without things getting out of hand. But the period of relative calm was short-lived. In the past few weeks William's angry outbursts have become more frequent again, and there have been serious arguments between William and Adam.

Although the parents have seen relapses like this before, this is different. Adam has subtle ways of provoking William's anger. He makes scornful remarks when they are together, and has learned how to badger William during meals. He makes remarks about noisy eating, kicks him under the table and steals food from his plate. The parents talk to Adam and try to make him understand how mean his behaviour is. When their efforts prove unsuccessful, their emotions quickly go from anger to despair until something finally breaks. They have worked on William's behaviour for years and were finally starting to see results. And now in just a few weeks Adam has succeeded in destroying everything they had achieved. He should know better!

They have learned from helping William that getting angry themselves does not help. Severe punishments and shouting are not the answer either. But what can they do? They feel so angry and desperate. The mother finds herself wishing she could spend a few weeks away from her family. Someplace where she can relax and there is no whining, arguing, shouting or other unpleasantness. Let them fend for themselves for awhile. Let them beat each other up!

A child who seriously misbehaves at home or in the classroom costs a great deal of energy. The adults have to conquer not only their own frustration, but also muster enough energy to carry out and maintain a behavioural programme. If you succeed in improving the child's level of functioning, you will be rewarded accordingly. You will be tired but proud of what you have accomplished. If the behavioural problems returns, it is very difficult to tap that same source of energy again. It is comparable to running a marathon. If you are mentally prepared for it, and can find the right cadence, you can run for a long time. But once you have crossed the finish line, you will not be able to run another race again until you have had time for rest, relaxation and recovery. It takes a while for your batteries to recharge for the next race. Even trained athletes cannot be expected to run a marathon every week without it taking a toll.

The parents in this portrait are taken aback when they find out that Adam is provoking William's inappropriate behaviour. After several attempts to reason with Adam they realise that they cannot bring him to his senses. They imagine the worst. Apparently they now have two children with behavioural problems. How will they cope? Can they expect more of the same when Charlotte reaches puberty? What are they doing wrong? Could it be hereditary? They dread the reactions of the rest of the family, with their well-intentioned advice... They are extremely frustrated about having lost control yet again. And they are so very tired.

The behavioural programme described in this book catches up with frustrated parents at precisely this point, the point at which they have run out of new ideas. The point they reach after they have tried everything and are forced to recognise that the problem is so complex that they don't know where to start. The more or less deadlocked situation is our starting point. These situations are often complex and difficult to describe, but describing your frustration is where the programme starts for you. The description is part of mapping out the situation, the first step of the behavioural programme. You start your strategy here but this time Adam is the subject, not William.

3. The cautious vice principal

Portrait of an older child

"The autonomous radical"

To say that Jacob is difficult is an understatement. In their meetings the teachers at his secondary school refer to him as an autonomous radical. The vice principal admits he has no control over Jacob. He does whatever he likes, is a frequent truant, smokes cannabis almost every day, does no homework and often shows up late for school. He is headed for disaster if he carries on like this. The hardest thing for the vice principal to accept is that he cannot talk to Jacob. At least not about his behaviour or the need to start working. Jacob, however, has a great deal to say about global warming, police brutality and the difference between smoking cannabis and drinking. If he is sent to the vice principal for breaking the school rules, Jacob explains at length why the rules are wrong, and how they are destroying students' creativity. He tells the vice principal that he can do as he likes, but that he, Jacob has no intention of staying after school or picking up rubbish in the schoolyard. Jacob feels no responsibility or concern for the people around him. It's their problem if they have trouble accepting his behaviour. The most the vice principal can expect from him is a lecture on how "uncool" it all is.

Jacob's behaviour is indeed very independent. But if he wants to function in a football team, a school or even in a group of autonomous radicals, he will have to learn how to deal with rules. For the time being, Jacob thinks he is justified in ignoring all rules, and doing his level best to avoid any discussion of this. He stymies all efforts to communicate with him on subjects not of his own choosing.

However, it is clear that he wants to be treated with respect. It is essential to use growth-promoting language when addressing this adolescent. Growth-promoting language shows respect. But if you say to him that you "no longer wish to treat him like a baby", he will not respond to this. There is no leverage here. "Whatever".

Jacob does not participate in the battle; he sidesteps it. He will interpret his own confrontation with boundaries as the adults' desire to pick a fight. Jacob is determined to avoid living by anyone else's rules. He is unaware of the fact that this type of communication makes him as vulnerable as a hedgehog curled up into a ball. If you want to address Jacob in growth-promoting language you will have to take not only his need for autonomy into account but also this vulnerability.

The vice principal knows that it will not be easy to hold a pro-active conversation. He opts for a combination of growth-promoting language and imagery. During the work session, he gives Jacob a compliment about the courage he shows in his attempts to mould his own life. "It's as if you have built a tall building all on your own. That is an enormous challenge." What the vice principal is saying is that while it is his job to hold Jacob to the school rules, he respects what Jacob has built for himself. The vice principal then announces that they are bound to disagree sometimes about the rules the school imposes on all of its students. He is very short and clear about the enforcement of these rules, but then he repeats his respect for what Jacob has singlehandedly built for himself.

One of two things can happen at this point. Jacob may become interested because he is being shown respect for his independent thinking, in which case there is a greater chance that a certain level of trust can be created. However, Jacob may also retreat further into an unapproachable attitude. The vice principal should not consider himself beaten. Jacob has heard what he said, but his defences are still intact. The vice principal can say that it is clear that they are still not in agreement, but that he sees that Jacob is working hard to mould his own life. He then indicates what the sanction is.

During every subsequent confrontation, Jacob will now know that the vice principal makes a distinction between him as an individual and his inappropriate behaviour. Dealing with Jacob and his behaviour in this fashion does not give the vice principal any guarantee that Jacob will respect the rules. It does make it possible for him to treat Jacob with respect and at the same time make it clear that there are limits to what the school can accept. He gives Jacob – who has a pronounced need for autonomy – the opportunity to choose but he also confronts him, in a friendly manner, with the consequences of his choice.

Jacob's school performance is below his intellectual capacity. He does not have to do very much, but in fact he does nothing at all. He does no homework and plays truant, but he continues to protest against those who enforce the rules. As a result he is often sent out of the classroom to the vice principal's office. The vice principal has decided against giving Jacob more severe punishment because he does not think he learns anything from it. It would probably only lead to Jacob's deciding to leave school altogether.

The vice principal has brief contact with Jacob during those moments when he has been kicked out of class. He now suggests meeting Jacob at the end of every school week, at twelve o'clock on Friday afternoon, for a ten-minute work session. Initially, they talk about the reasons for his exclusion from the class, or about the type of teacher who is not good at dealing with Jacob's behaviour. The vice principal gradually steers the conversations towards Jacob's plans for the future. They have a good laugh about his get-rich-quick schemes. The vice principal cannot help himself. He says, "You should stay at school another year, Jacob. You'll be even better prepared to make even more money." The vice principal does not know whether these talks were effective, but he is certainly relieved when Jacob squeaks by and passes his final exams.

4. The partial intervention in a complex situation

Portrait of an older child

"Fraternal conflict"

Aaron is 16 years old and his brother Jamie is 17. They used to get along together very well but now that they are older they fight almost every day. Sometimes it gets physical and their father has to intervene. Aaron calls his 19-year old sister Rachel a whore. She refuses to accept this and shouts back at him. Mealtimes are not pleasant. The parents have their hands full, and it is almost impossible to sit down together at the table without the threat of physical violence.

What is wrong? The parents do not understand why the situation is always so explosive. At first they thought Jamie was secretly smoking cannabis and that this made him irritable. Or maybe it was the fact that Aaron is dyslectic and had trouble keeping up at school. And Rachel had become increasingly vocal. Was that the reason?

For the parents it is frustrating that their children treat one another this way. They apologise after every incident but soon fall into the same patterns of behaviour again. The boys goad one another, as if they had some score to settle. It is so bad that the parents are afraid to leave Aaron and Jamie alone together in the house. They find it impossible to reason with them.

The parents are now convinced that it is time for a different approach. They decide to stop the never-ending rounds of discussion and interrogation. Talking about matters is evidently no longer an option. You would think they were dealing with angry toddlers.

Jamie is irritable after losing a football match on Saturday afternoon. The parents foresee problems during dinner, and they announce that Jamie will have to eat in his room. But Jamie is not about to give up his privileged position as troublemaker at the table without a fight. He says his parents are childish and he refuses to cooperate. His mother says she agrees that it is childish and hopes it will not be necessary for long. "But we are doing what we said we would do, and that is the end of the discussion." When it is time for dinner, Jamie starts to sit down at the table. His mother calmly prepares a plate for him and takes it up to his room. When she comes back into the kitchen she tells him in a friendly manner that his dinner is waiting for him in his room. Jamie understands that she means what she says and he goes off to his room, quietly swearing under his breath. Aaron eats in silence.

The mother has given the correct response to Jamie's attempt to take back control. When she says that she also thinks it is childish that this intervention is necessary, she is showing decisiveness. But she is also subtly indicating that this is the consequence of his own childish behaviour; she hopes that the intervention will not have to last long. This is wording that prevents a loss of face for Jamie, but the message is still loud and clear.

However, that is not the end of it. Jamie makes a second attempt to undermine his mother's authority by simply sitting down at the table. She does what she said she would do, and refuses to be drawn into an argument. Jamie's father supports her by not letting his son provoke him. His mother takes his plate up to his room. There is no need for comment. The mother passes the test, and the message is clear to Jamie. If he wants a hot meal he had better go to his room right now.

In this family we see different behaviours that require an intervention. Calling Rachel names, being too quick to anger and to react to one another's behaviour at the table, and the boys' fighting are examples of this. If the intervention is evaluated in terms of the method described in the book, we see that it is not perfect. The announcement could have been made at a more pro-active moment. The boys' mother could make more use of growth-promoting language, and she forgets the post-active intervention. However, even though it was incomplete, this intervention worked. This is something you often see as the work attitude of the relevant adults changes from passive to active. As their work attitude becomes more active, parents also become more adept at using the method. This makes it easier for them to prepare the interventions for the problems on their list.

The intervention was geared to the lower level at which Jamie functions. The parents accept that Jamie is unable to give an age appropriate response to losing his football match. He will take out his frustration on Aaron, and although that can happen anywhere in the house, they choose mealtime for the intervention. They are just in time to pro-actively announce that Jamie will be eating in his room this evening. It is a good idea to do this together, if possible. The intervention consists of a time out during the family meal. The message to Jamie is clear: if he wants to be treated like a 17-year old at the table, he will have to meet certain conditions.

This intervention was used for Jamie, but Aaron and Rachel know full well that it might be their turn next time. The children see that their parents have formed a united front and taken a very firm stance. They were accustomed to seeing their parents give the "guilty" party a good dressing down. All they had to do was listen and apologise. Now their parents appear to have changed tack. There is no more talking. The advantage for the parents is that all three children now have to meet certain conditions if they want to enjoy a family meal together.

5. When no programme works

Portrait of an older child

"Dropping out of the programme"
The parents of 16-year old Harry have been concerned about him for a long time. Does he have ADHD or some other disorder? Why is it so difficult to get him to go to school? Is he on drugs? Why does he sit in his room all day and only come to life when his girlfriend comes around? The parents have many questions and do not know which approach they should take. How can they get him back on track? '

Harry's room is completely chaotic, and even he no longer knows where to find things. He resists all efforts to clean it. His mother has now said she will tidy and clean the room at least once a month. Once the room is clean Harry is pleased that everything smells fresh again and that his clothes are stacked neatly in the closet. But he never manages to keep it that way for more than a day. His parents have gone through the various stages of despair.

Several different plans have already failed. A plan to fine Harry 50 cents every time he throws his clothes on the floor instead of in the laundry basket seems like a good idea. The amount is to be deducted from his pocket money. However, the parents notice that the plan has no effect whatsoever. Harry is apparently unconcerned about his pocket money. He offers no solution for the resulting deficit, and makes absolutely no effort to put his laundry in the basket.

Another plan also quickly fails. The parents decide to start with something small by encouraging Harry to pack his school bag the night before. It would be so much easier if he did not have to look for his things at the last minute. If he gets out of bed at all, it is at the very last minute, and it is very difficult to find things in such a messy room. There are usually scenes in the morning, and Harry is often late for school. Harry refuses to participate in this stupid programme. He thinks home is more like a prison. His parents are on the verge of despair.

Harry's parents see that their son's level of functioning is very low. Evidently they cannot expect a behavioural intervention to give them any leverage. No matter what they do, Harry drops out of the training programme. They have reached an impasse, in which there is no programme in place at all. What can they try next, and how can they restore their own work attitude?

Harry's parents decide not to undertake any training programme at all for the time being. They accept that he functions at an even lower level than they thought. They decide that one of them will pack his bag, keep his bookcase tidy, and clean his room every week. Actually, this is what they would do if Harry was sick. Harry can call this ridiculous if he wants, and make comments about how his parents are acting like slaves. He can argue with his parents with a view to making them angry and passive again. But his parents are not having it. They make it very clear in advance what they are going to do and for how long. The parents agree that they will follow their new strategy until Harry gets back into the programme. Every week they will hold a work session with him to determine whether he is capable of taking over one or more small tasks.

This may seem like a dangerous tactic on the part of the parents. The new situation might suit Harry very well. But it is a relatively small investment that will improve the circumstances surrounding the need to get Harry off to school every day. And the micro climate in his room will improve.

The parents' plan is also strategic. They are introducing an intervention that clarifies the real problem:
- Harry may eventually get tired of being treated as if he is sick and start doing a few things himself. It will be easier for him to do this because his starting point will no longer be as completely chaotic as it was before.
- It may also be that while he is tired of his role as a sick person, the pressure it creates may make it clear to him what the problem is. This process may uncover unexpected and surprising underlying reasons for his behaviour, such as an undetected learning disability or a traumatic experience. He may have problems with his sexual identity or a deeper developmental problem. In that case the parents may want to seek professional help.
- Finally, it may also become clear that Harry has no interest at all in cooperating. The question then is whether it is still possible for him to live at home. The parents can consider a boarding school, or some other type of supervised living arrangement. But they can also decide to keep Harry at home and hope that at some point things will improve.

This portrait is not encouraging. But it does show you that it is possible to devise a programme even for a child who functions at a very low level. The important thing for you, the adult, is to maintain an active work attitude in the post-active phase, and to keep asking yourself: does the programme work or do I need to change something?

By staying alert and drawing the conclusion that in many areas "nothing works", you realise that it is time to take stock of the situation again. It is nearly always the case that the child is functioning at a very low level. Sometimes at a level that it so low that no training programme is effective. This no-nonsense conclusion is the result of having systematically followed all of the steps of this programme. It leads to the clear decision that this child requires a different approach.

E. Quick Reference Section

Coming to grips with children's inappropriate behaviour: Summary

1. Take stock of the inappropriate behaviour: what frustrates you? How long has the problem existed? Which situations are the most emotional? Who is in charge? Can the situation be allowed to continue?

2. Check your own work attitude and repair it if necessary: are you in a passive or an active position? Make a project out of this!

3. Make a list containing exact descriptions of the inappropriate behaviours: describe what you see.

4. Choose one project from the list: if necessary, divide it into categories and sub-categories.

5. Evaluate the child's level of functioning. If it is low, choose a method based on scaling back inappropriate behaviour.

6. When devising an intervention, think carefully about your approach to the child.

7. Make good use of timing: take the pressure off the reactive moment by making better use of the pro-active and post-active moments.

8. Base your actions on the child's level of functioning: connect with him at that level, not at an age-appropriate level.

9. Hold a pro-active work session with the child. Use growth-promoting language and tell the child what will happen if he behaves inappropriately. Agree on the warning signal you will give. Consider using a process box for older children.

10. Give the warning signal as soon as inappropriate behaviour occurs.

11. If the behaviour recurs or does not stop within the agreed period of time, impose a sanction. Sanctions often take the form of a time out.

12. After the sanction, welcome the child using growth-promoting language. Make a brief statement that links the current situation to the next practice situation.

13. If the inappropriate behaviour recurs, be consistent about issuing a warning and imposing another sanction.

14. Once you have seen sufficient improvement of the relevant behaviour, move on to the next item on the list. Do not lose momentum when the first phase of the programme is finished.

APPENDICES

1. Map out the situation	1.1. Give a general description of the inappropriate behaviour	1.1.a. Identifying the source of frustration
		1.1.b. Describing the course of behaviour over time
	1.2. Describe your current response and emotions	1.2.a. Reviewing the role of the child in the problem
		1.2.b. Reviewing the role of the adults in the problem
		1.2.c. Reviewing the role of the environment in the problem
	1.3. Ask yourself who is in charge	1.3.a. Reviewing the role of the child
		1.3.b. Reviewing the role of the adult
	1.4. Describe your concerns and your hopes	1.4.a. Checking short-term consequences
		1.4.b. Checking long-term consequences
	1.5. Determine whether the current situation can be allowed to continue	1.5.a. Draw conclusions
		1.5.b. Setting a time limit
		1.5.c. Setting a limit with regard to an acceptable level of functioning
2. Fix your own attitude first	2.1. Identify your attitude	2.1.a. Drawing a distinction between your attitude and the work floor
		2.1.b. Identifying the vicious circle
	2.2. Go from passive to active	2.2.a. Accepting the chronic nature of the problems
		2.2.b. Redefining unwillingness as inability
		2.2.c. Going from waiting to starting a project
3. Prepare the intervention	3.1. Choose the behaviour that needs to change	3.1.a. Making a list
		3.1.b. Choosing a category and subcategory
		3.1.c. Determining the level of functioning
	3.2. Design the intervention	3.2.a. Basing the intervention on the level of functioning
		3.2.b. Timing the intervention
		3.2.c. Shaping the intervention
4. Hold a work session using growth-promoting language	4.1. Announce the work session	4.1.a. Inviting the child
		4.1.b. Determining the conditions
	4.2. Hold the work session	4.2.a. Using growth-promoting language
		4.2.b. Giving a brief explanation of your reasons
		4.2.c. Announcing the sanction
	4.3. Conclude the work session	4.3.a. Being prepared for resistance
		4.3.b. Staying in control
5. Apply the sanction	5.1. Give the announced sign	5.1.a. Avoiding delay
		5.1.b. Avoiding further discussion
	5.2. Apply the sanction calmly and professionally	5.2.a. Meaning what you say
		5.2.b. Avoiding an angry response
		5.2.c. Sticking to the time schedule
	5.3. Deal with new inappropriate behaviour	5.3.a. Dealing with the child's contribution to the problem
		5.3.b. Dealing with the adult's contribution to the problem
6. Use growth-promoting language to evaluate the intervention	6.1. Be aware of the need to hold an appraisal	6.1.a. Recognising the appraisal as part of the programme
		6.1.b. Understanding the advantages of the appraisal
	6.2. Maintain an active work attitude	6.2.a. Staying alert
		6.2.b. Using the coaching model
		6.2.c. Understanding the power of repetition
	6.3. Discuss the child's reaction to the sanction in growth promoting language	6.3.a. Avoiding the you-bin
		6.3.b. Using positive wording
	6.4. Link one practice situation to the next	6.4.a. Making the post-active appraisal pro-active
		6.4.b. Maintaining focus

www.ingramcontent.com/pod-product-compliance
Ingram Content Group UK Ltd.
Pitfield, Milton Keynes, MK11 3LW, UK
UKHW050416240426
12048UKWH00021B/1539